A Program for Teaching Social Literacy

Deborah Prothrow-Stith
Joseph M. Chéry
Jon Oliver

with Clementina Chéry
Marci Feldman
Fern Shamis

GRADES K-1 | TEACHER'S GUIDE

Research Press
2612 North Mattis Avenue • Champaign, Illinois 61822
(800) 519-2707 • www.researchpress.com

Composition by Jeff Helgesen
Cover design by Linda Brown, Positive I.D. Graphic Design, Inc.
Illustrations by Karen Samatis
Printed by Bang Printing, Inc.

ISBN 0–87822–502–1
Library of Congress Control Number 2004113185

For all who dare to dream a world without violence

Contents

Foreword

In a world where new reports of terrible violence make the news every evening—some half a world away, some as close as the town or home next door—teaching our children how to prevent violence is essential. I am so grateful for this curriculum, which provides a fine blueprint for change. I applaud the teachers, community leaders, and parents who read it and decide that change will start with them. Indeed, change has to start with each one of us if our children are to learn how to relate to one another in peaceable ways, without violence.

Studies have long shown that the keys to preventing violence by and against young people require minimizing the factors that contribute to aggressive and violent behaviors and maximizing the protective factors that help reduce violence by young people and those close to them. According to the U.S. Census Bureau, nearly seven million children are left home alone after school each week. In this time, between the hours of 3 P.M. and 6 P.M., troublesome behavior is most likely to happen. Without adult supervision, young people are at risk of engaging in dangerous behavior. Youths who participate in good after-school and youth development programs are less likely to use drugs, drink alcohol, smoke, or become sexually active. They are more likely to have stronger interpersonal skills, higher academic achievement, and healthier relationships with others. This means they are less likely to engage in violent behaviors, get into trouble, and hurt others.

We must challenge political leaders who repeatedly attempt to cut federal funding for after-school, vocational education, and other programs that effectively provide at-risk youths needed supervision and positive alternatives to the street and negative peer pressure. And we must insist that *all* youth who need such programs be served. But research and experience show there are other proven ways to instill values that help keep youth out of trouble, which is why resources like the Peacezone curriculum are so important.

This resource *works* and has the potential to teach thousands of children skills they need and will use again and again in their everyday lives. Arguments, jealousy, frustration, and loss of self-control are common emotions to children and adults everywhere. What's different, however, is how so many young people act out these feelings. A police officer interviewed in a recent *Washington Post* column shared how he and his partner, in a routine patrol, pulled over a fourteen-year-old boy driving without a seatbelt or license and discovered a loaded Mac-11 semiautomatic handgun and .380 semiautomatic pistol in the car. This young teen was stopped in the same neighborhood where the police officer had grown up, and the thirty-year-old officer wondered, "What is a fourteen-year-old doing with this kind of firepower? We weren't into guns when I was growing up, unless we were playing cowboys with cap guns. Firearms were off limits. Kids my age just didn't see guns. But this younger generation is different. Every day that I'm on the street, I expect to face juveniles who are armed. And I know what a fourteen-year-old is capable of. . . . When you're that young and facing adult situations, you're going to make a lot of wrong decisions."

"For many of these young people," he added, "a firearm is like money. It makes you powerful. You can use it to collect so many things the wrong way. A kid with a gun can take a vehicle. He can take someone's livelihood or his manhood or his life. The person who gets violated may want to retaliate, but if he doesn't have a gun, he's not capable. The one with the gun feels immortal, as if life is stopping for him."

Disgracefully, our nation and too many adults have made it far too easy for guns and other violent weapons to get into children's hands. The results have tragically affected multiple generations. A child or teen is killed by guns every three hours. It's time to stop the proliferation of guns and the increasingly lethal nature of violence. It's time to teach our children other ways to feel and to be powerful and in control, ways that don't involve hurting others or themselves. It's time to teach and support our children in making right decisions in right ways—nonviolent ways. It's time for adults to accept our responsibility to provide our children with new tools—compelling enough for young people to choose them instead of guns. Teachers will find these kinds of tools in this fine curriculum.

An important point to remember about the Peacezone curriculum is that it is not just for children already causing trouble. It is not just for inner-city children or poor children or somebody else's children. Its lessons are for *all* children. All children need self-control and self-respect. All children need to learn how to cooperate and solve problems nonviolently. And all children need adults who model and teach behavior that respects diversity and displays a positive attitude. These values need to be instilled in every classroom and home and practiced with peers across the range of experiences all young people share.

Louis Brown's tragic death reminds us that violence affects us all. Children brought up in homes that teach positive values and nonviolence must share neighborhoods and streets and a nation with children denied these crucial foundations and left to fend for themselves. I hope a curriculum like this one becomes a required and integral part of every child's education across our nation. Teaching nonviolence to all our children will help ensure a safe world for all of us. If children are safe, everybody's safe.

A recent article on the power of the Peacezone training described a session in the spring of 2003 that took place the day the United States began bombing Baghdad, Iraq. Participating children ranged from kindergartners through fifth graders. They wanted to have a serious discussion about what kinds of skills they thought President Bush and Secretary of State Powell were and were not using during their "peace" talks. One student, Angel, asked why U.S. and Iraqi leaders couldn't have done what he was being taught to do: "I wonder why they couldn't just talk it over instead of having wars?"

It's time for adults to answer Angel's question. All children and adults have much to learn from programs like the Peacezone. Mohandas K. Gandhi correctly stressed that "if we are to teach real peace in this world, and if we are to carry on a real war against war, we shall have to begin with the children."

MARIAN WRIGHT EDELMAN
FOUNDER AND PRESIDENT
CHILDREN'S DEFENSE FUND

Program Partners

The Peacezone curriculum is the result of a partnership among three organizations: Harvard School of Public Health, Lesson One Company, and the Louis D. Brown Peace Institute.

Harvard School of Public Health

Harvard School of Public Health (HSPH) has extensive experience conducting continuing education, training, and evaluation. Founded in 1922, the school grew out of the Harvard–MIT School for Health Officers, the nation's first graduate training program in public health. In its first fifty years, the HSPH was responsible for many landmark contributions to public health. The HSPH Division of Public Health Practice houses violence prevention programs under the direction of founding director, Dr. Deborah Prothrow-Stith. Dr. Prothrow-Stith, author of the Violence Prevention Curriculum for Adolescents used in schools in all 50 United States, has traveled across the country addressing audiences representing professionals—including educators and others involved in our nation's schools—and community members, helping them understand the epidemic of violence and encouraging them to develop violence prevention initiatives in their schools and communities.

Harvard School of Public Health
677 Huntington Avenue
Boston, MA 02115
Phone: 617–495–7777
Web site: www.hsph.harvard.edu

Lesson One Company

Lesson One Company has been providing educational services to schools and families in Boston, Massachusetts, surrounding communities, and nationwide since 1976. During that time, Lesson One programs have evolved to meet the changing needs of youth while continually focusing on prevention of violence and other risky behaviors. Developed through the feedback of thousands of teachers, school administrators, and parents/guardians, Lesson One's ABCs of Life program is designed for educators to instill basic social and emotional skills in their students. The philosophy, concepts, and strategies of the ABCs of Life program are based on years of practical experience and research. The program has been presented to schools in 20 states and is now available to all who live and work with children in the book

Lesson One: The ABCs of Life—The Skills We All Need but Were Never Taught
(Simon and Schuster, 2004). A cornerstone of the program is to teach children the relationship between school and life, a principle often posited in theory but seldom expressed in practice.

Lesson One Company
245 Newbury Street, Suite 2F
Boston, MA 02116
Phone: 617–247–2787
Web site: www.lessonone.org

Louis D. Brown Peace Institute

The mission of the Louis D. Brown Peace Institute is to develop programs that encourage young people to promote peace and social justice, and to empower survivors of homicide victims with tools that rebuild their lives and communities through education, collaboration, and policy advocacy. The institute is named for fifteen-year-old peacemaker Louis David Brown, who dreamed of becoming the first black president of the United States. Joseph and Clementina Chéry, the parents of Louis D. Brown, founded the institute in 1994, after their son was killed in a senseless act of gang violence. It seeks to achieve its mission by developing programs that encourage young people to avoid violence and by creating activities that instill values and enrich the lives of youth. The institute teaches the value of peace to students in grades K–12 through three peace curricula: the Louis D. Brown Peace Curriculum for High Schools, Connecting In-School and After-School Activities for Middle Schools, and Peacemaker's ABC for Elementary Schools.

Louis D. Brown Peace Institute
Second Floor
1452 Dorchester Avenue
Dorchester, MA 02122
Phone: 617–825–1917
Web site: www.institute4peace.org/institute

Acknowledgments

Our sincere thanks to the Peacezone curriculum development team: Rita Colavincenzo, Ameera Crellin, Steve Morrissey, Olive Prince, Laura Privitera, Laura Root, Roland Smart, Blue Telusma, and LeSette Wright. Your hard work and commitment were vital to the development of this project. We owe special thanks to Blue Telusma and Nancy O'Keefe Bolick, both of the Louis D. Brown Peace Institute, for contributing stories to the curriculum, and to LeSette Wright, of the Harvard School of Public Health, for coordinating the efforts of the authors and for contributing the appendix describing Peacezone healing skills activities and resources.

The Peacezone curriculum was improved significantly through a host of expert recommendations and critical review. We are grateful for this group of assiduous professionals:

Thomas Menino
Mayor, City of Boston

U.S. Department of Education
Office of Safe and Drug-Free Schools

Thomas Payzant
Boston Public Schools

Jay Silverman, Ph.D.
Harvard School of Public Health

Bruce Kennedy, Ph.D.
Harvard School of Public Health

Barbara Oehlberg
The National Institute for Trauma and Loss in Children

We extend our thanks to the following Massachusetts school principals, teachers, and students: Principal Jean Dorcus, Principal Cheryl Watson-Harris, Principal Craig Lankhorst, Principal Dr. Robert Martin, Principal John Waggett, Georgie Chavez, Tracey Nicolazzo, Mike Lawrence-Riddle, Selena Quirindongo, Rochelle Weeks, Joan Rego, Marjorie Schneider, and Regina White-Jones.

Thanks also go to the staff and faculty of the following schools: Haley Elementary School, Kenny Elementary School, Fifield Elementary School, O'Donnell Elementary School, Farragut Elementary School, Otis Elementary School, Dickerman Elementary School, and Winthrop Elementary School.

Special thanks to the Boston Public Schools and Superintendent Thomas Payzant for their participation in the development and pilot testing of the curriculum. The success of this project is also due in large part to the Department of Education, Office of Safe and Drug-Free Schools, which provided funding for development and pilot testing of the curriculum.

Introduction

Congratulations on choosing the Peacezone curriculum. This Teacher's Guide and the Student Manual that accompanies it are the product of cooperation among the Harvard School of Public Health, Lesson One Company, and the Louis D. Brown Institute. The goal of our collaboration is to help you help your students promote peace, improve their behavior, and overcome challenging issues associated with grief and violence.

More specifically, the primary mission of the Peacezone program is to increase the ability of children to promote peace, make positive decisions, and avoid risk-taking behaviors. To achieve this goal, the program depends on three key concepts:

1. The innate strength and resiliency of youth

2. The importance of addressing the grief and loss issues that play a key role in the choices children make

3. The importance of life skills and their effect on students not only in their school lives, but also in their homes and communities

We believe that children exposed to the Peacezone program will display positive behavior outcomes and will learn, understand, use, and internalize the major concepts of the program.

Although you may choose to use this curriculum within individual classrooms or an entire school, the Peacezone program is a climate-change mechanism: Use of this curriculum will have an impact on the climate of your classroom and school as students internalize program principles, making teachers and students proud of themselves and their community.

Fundamentals for Teachers

All children have a right to feel safe. We know that if children don't feel safe, it is more difficult for them to learn. It is important for children to understand that no one can feel truly safe unless those around them feel safe as well. From talking to countless teachers and students, it appears that many children do not feel safe in home and school environments and that these feelings of fear influence their behavior negatively throughout the day.

One of the key components of the Peacezone program is the acknowledgment that feelings of grief and loss play a key role in the choices children make. Sometimes it can be difficult for adults to know how a child is coping with feelings of grief and loss. This is especially true for children who are relatively uncommunicative, shy, and/or afraid. To aid children in their healing process, adults must learn to recognize signs of children's grief and understand that children process and respond to loss in various ways. Since children take their cues in how to deal with many situations from adults, it is important for adults to be sensitive to their own grief processes, needs, and feelings. As a teacher of this curriculum, your thoughts regarding violence, grief, and loss may be challenged.

In the first unit of the Peacezone program, you will be addressing issues relating to safety, grief, and loss through the story of Louis D. Brown. Louis D. Brown was a fifteen-year-old peace-maker who was the innocent victim of a gang shooting in 1993. Louis wanted all children to be safe and to reach their dreams. To prepare for this inspirational story, the program explores the issue of safety with children and gives them an opportunity to reflect on what safe and unsafe environments feel like.

Throughout the school day, encourage your students to respond to transitions and other significant classroom routines within the framework of safety. These are teachable moments that often escape us as educators. Affirm peacemaking behaviors within this framework by commenting on how the class moved to the library, for example, in a way that allowed everyone to feel safe and comfortable. Refer to behaviors that do not enhance the overall sense of safety as being exactly that. Ask or comment on whether or not the rest of the class felt at ease when the noise level around the resource table or reading corner was very high. The following discussion will help you with this process.

Overview of the Curriculum

The main components of the Peacezone curriculum are this Teacher's Guide and the Student Manual. Most other materials required are readily available in most classrooms: chalkboard or easel pad, drawing paper and crayons or markers, writing paper, and so forth. When other materials or props are called for, these are listed in the lesson.

Teacher's Guide

This Teacher's Guide is divided into the following Peacezone units:

Unit 1: Louis D. Brown

Unit 2: Pledge for Peace

Unit 3: Trying Your Best

Unit 4: Self-Control

Unit 5: Thinking and Problem Solving

Unit 6: Cooperation

Throughout the units are lessons with discussion starters, games, activities, project ideas, stories, and home pages. Some of these lessons include photocopiable activity pages so teachers may collect, review, and display students' work. We also include a variety of community service activities to help students transfer their knowledge of the skills into everyday practice.

The games and activities that are a part of each unit are designed for ease of replication. They are all success oriented and noncompetitive, so all students will be able to participate and learn from them.

Student Manual

As a supplement to this book, each student will have an illustrated Peacezone Student Manual. When used with other program instruction and activities, these manuals help ensure that students fully understand and have a lasting record of lesson content. The manuals are illustrated and include a variety of hands-on activities to promote students' understanding and application of Peacezone principles. In it, students draw, write, and work together to solve problems.

Appendixes to the Teacher's Guide

Appendix A: Program Theory and Evaluation

These pages provide an explanation of the basis of the Peacezone program in the theories of intrapersonal and interpersonal intelligences and the ecological model of health promotion. In addition, they explain formative evaluation of the program and detail the positive results of outcome evaluations.

Appendix B: Louis D. Brown Story (Adult Version)

The adult version of the Louis D. Brown story, written by Nancy O'Keefe Bolick (of the Louis D. Brown Peace Institute), gives teachers and others interested in program implementation a broader view of Louis's story. With this context, they are more able to explain and elicit student responses from the version included for students in Unit 1.

Appendix C: Peacezone Posters

This appendix provides full-page examples of information to be presented in whole-class format: the Pledge for Peace and the Peacezone skills (Trying Your Best, Self-Control, Thinking and Problem Solving, and Cooperation), as well as other important program content. You may photocopy and distribute these pages to students, other teachers, or parents; enlarge them; or create your own posters—on your own or with the help of your students.

Appendix D: Peacezone Home Pages

The Home Pages summarize the content of the Peacezone program, unit by unit, to communicate program goals and encourage the support of parents or guardians.

Appendix E: Healing Skills—Activities and Resources

This appendix provides information and activities concerning some of the interpersonal connections between violence and other issues, such as grief, loss, anger, and fear. Teachers and students are often interested in exploring these connections further. We recognize that additional information is required in order to enhance this aspect of curriculum implementation.

Daily Steps for Building Safe Peacezones

1. Appreciate every person's right to be safe.

2. Establish what being safe feels like (physically and emotionally).

3. Explore and develop guidelines that make it possible for every person in the classroom to feel safe.

4. Refer to disruptions or inappropriate behaviors as upsetting the sense of safety for the entire class.

5. Discuss what needs to happen so a sense of safety, if missing, can be restored.

The lessons and strategies included in the Peacezone curriculum are tools to help you and your class make your classroom a "peace zone." Please think of the program as an environment rather than a set of individual lessons. The concepts of the Peacezone program can be discussed during a math or history lesson, or in the course of daily interactions among teachers, students, and parents.

We know the demands on teachers are many. The Peacezone curriculum is not an attempt to further burden teachers. Rather, our research has demonstrated that using the curriculum improves student behavior, providing more time for teachers to teach and requiring less time for discipline, as program evaluations have shown.

Frequently Asked Questions

Are some children too young to hear Louis's story?

Most children have already been exposed to violence. If the exposure is not direct (e.g., in the home or community), children have certainly been exposed to violence through the media, including TV, movies, daily news programs, and video games. Given this exposure to violence and death, teachers must work with parents to use developmentally appropriate language and activities to help children process death, sadness, loss, and pain. The Peacezone was created for this purpose.

A child's reaction to grief, loss, and other trauma will likely vary depending on his or her emotional and developmental stage. Children of primary school age are capable of understanding simple, concrete explanations, but they have not yet acquired abstract reasoning abilities. The Peacezone program works with children to process grief and loss at the appropriate developmental level, strengthening children's communication and life skills.

How do I handle the emotional reactions some children may have to Louis's story?

We do not expect teachers to be therapists. If a child has a severe or long-term reaction, don't be afraid to ask for help. If your school does not have a counselor or psychologist on site, call your district office to ask for support. Also, keep in mind that your local community may have resources available to you and your students. Many children do not need intensive therapy. Rather, we suggest that you do what you do on a regular basis: Listen to the concerns of your students and provide comfort and support. Give your student choices. Having choices encourages students' sense of self-control and increases their feeling of safety.

How does trauma affect children's school performance?

It is not unusual for traumatized children to show a decline in school performance and attendance. When children lack a sense of safety and security, it is difficult to focus on learning. Studies by researchers such as Dr. Bruce Perry, of the Child Trauma Academy in Houston, also suggest that trauma affects brain development.

Will the Pledge for Peace become rote if it is read aloud every day?

No, the Pledge for Peace will not become rote if the appropriate supporting activities are also implemented. Although reading the entire pledge does not take up a significant amount of time, you may want to shorten it further by focusing on only one item in the pledge each time you read it. You can tell a story about how you may have been challenged by an area in the pledge, or you can have students share a story from their lives. In addition, individual children or groups of children can recite the Pledge for Peace during a given week. Finally, we suggest that teachers refer to the pledge throughout the day as the opportunity arises. This will make it a natural, not rote, part of the school day.

How does community service fit into the curriculum?

We include community service activities for several reasons. First, these activities help children apply the skills they have learned through the Peacezone program. Second, community service activities can be a healing process for those who have experienced violence in their lives. By doing for others, children are also helping themselves. Incorporate information about community or neighborhood incidents that involve violence into these discussions, especially when such incidents are common knowledge among students. Address national events as well, if you feel comfortable doing so. Explore what might help your students build a sense of safety in your classroom and school.

When is the best time of day to use the Peacezone skills?

Any time. Like the Pledge for Peace, you can refer to the skills throughout the school day. For example, if a student raises her hand instead of calling out, you can tell her what a great job she did using her self-control. The skills are everywhere. In current events, books, and history, you can point out which people are using or not using the skills. Teachable moments such as these bring the skills to life.

In particular, you can strengthen the skill of Self-Control in the following way: Tell students that they can practice their self-control by not touching instructional materials that you pass out until you have given directions. Explain that if they are not using their self-control, you will take the materials away. When they get their self-control back, you will return them. When a student who has lost his self-control regains it, he can feel proud.

My students, and sometimes their parents, say that it is unrealistic to try to avoid violence—that they don't really have a choice about fighting. What can I tell them?

First, ask students why they feel they don't have a real choice. Usually, what they really mean is either that the choices are unattractive (e.g., they involve losing face) or that they can't believe that nonviolent alternatives will really work. The latter is a common reaction of both teenagers and adults. One of the problems with nonviolent solutions is that they cannot, as a rule, be reduced to a simple, easily applied formula. In addition, the popular culture offers very few role models for nonviolence, and those that do exist are generally more applicable to political situations (e.g., Martin Luther King, Jr., and Mohandas K. Gandhi) than to the kinds of interpersonal conflict situations discussed in this curriculum. Second, ask the class for examples from their own experience: We all have more experience with nonviolent conflict resolution than we think we do. Finally, reaffirm that there is always a choice, and although students may well make the choice to fight, they should do so only after assessing the situation and not simply because they have lost their temper or can think of nothing else to do.

Saving face is a major concern with my students; it overrides everything else. How should I address this?

This issue is often difficult for teachers to understand because it points out one of the differences between adults and youths: Our students are likely to feel that their entire sense of self-esteem depends on the outcome of a particular conflict, whereas adults usually have a more long-range perspective.

As a rule, it is counterproductive to spend much time attempting to explain to students that walking away from a conflict is not an admission of weakness. They simply don't believe it. Instead, emphasize these ideas:

▶ Avoiding being put in the situation where losing face becomes an issue by recognizing the kind of behavior that leads to a fight

▶ Not letting anyone force you into a fight

▶ Assessing a conflict situation for what you want, not for what your opponent wants

▶ Weighing the risks and rewards of the available choices

How long will each lesson take me? Can I break up the lessons if necessary?

Each lesson will take forty-five minutes to one hour to complete. Some teachers find it easier to divide the lessons into two thirty-minute time slots, whereas others choose to stick to the one-hour slot. The Peacezone curriculum can be tailored to fit the needs of each individual classroom.

How do I know the curriculum is working?

Teachers may choose to assess their students using the following criteria: level of participation in class discussions, completion of assignments, evidence of careful thought about the ideas raised in discussions, retention of vocabulary, and use of skills. In addition, many teachers have asked students to keep journals to record notes about the lessons, as well as thoughts about and responses to the content of lessons.

I purchased the curriculum for my individual classroom. What support do I need to make it successful?

The Peacezone program is a school climate-change mechanism. If you are using the curriculum in your individual classroom, we encourage you to incorporate the language and philosophy of the program schoolwide. You can do this by sharing the Peacezone program with your building administrator, parent council, and colleagues. Promoting the Pledge for Peace as a schoolwide initiative will help your students internalize Peacezone skills while sharing program principles throughout the school community.

How should I use the healing skills?

Violence is intimately connected with issues of grief and loss, anger, and fear; frequently, teachers and students are interested in exploring these connections further. The healing skills activities and resource lists included in Appendix E can help your students internalize the Peacezone skills.

You may use this information in a variety of ways. For example, the activities related to grief and loss can be used in conjunction with the Louis D. Brown unit. Other healing skills activities complement the units on the Pledge for Peace and specific Peacezone skills (Trying Your Best, Self-Control, Thinking and Problem Solving, and Cooperation). The resource lists are helpful in gathering information for and designing additional activities to be used with students, parents, and school personnel.

Peacezone Curricula for Other Grade Levels

The Peacezone curriculum for grades K–1 is followed by two others—for grades 2–3 and 4–5, respectively. When you use the Peacezone program for any grade level, we suggest that you make each lesson your own—use your creativity and expertise to customize the information! Based upon the needs of your school, please feel free to extend, expand, or adapt the lessons described here to introduce students to the program.

Louis D. Brown

The Louis D. Brown story is the foundation of the Peacezone program. In this unit, you and your students will learn the inspiring story of an extraordinary young man, who, by setting a goal for himself and taking steps to realize his goal, gave hope to all young people in their ability to set and achieve their goals and dreams. Louis's life was tragically cut short by a stray bullet on a December day as he was preparing to attend a meeting of a group dedicated to peacemaking.

The story of Louis D. Brown is set in his home in Dorchester, Massachusetts, a neighborhood in Boston. The story describes his life at home and at school, his efforts to make the world a safer place, and his aspirations toward the presidency of the United States. Through Louis D. Brown, students learn the relevance of the Peacezone skills in their lives.

Before teaching the first lesson in this unit, take the time to read the Louis D. Brown story for adults (Appendix B) for background. Photocopy the Louis D. Brown poster in Appendix C or create a larger version of it to display on an easel pad or bulletin board. Hang the poster in your classroom in a place where everyone in class can see it.

You can provide students with a general introduction to the Peacezone program by following the steps on pages 13–14. Refer to the Louis D. Brown poster as you explain who Louis was and why he is important to the Peacezone program.

Introducing the Peacezone Program

OBJECTIVE Students will understand how Louis D. Brown's story relates to the Peacezone program.

MATERIALS ▶ Louis D. Brown poster (Appendix C)

PROCEDURE *Before teaching this lesson, hang the Louis D. Brown poster in a prominent location in your classroom. Leave the poster up for future reference.*

STEP 1 —— **Give the students some basic information about Louis D. Brown.**

You might say something like the following:

> Welcome to the Peacezone program. In this program, we will be learning about the life of Louis D. Brown. Throughout the year, we will be finding out about Louis and how his peacemaking skills can help us be safe.
>
> Louis was a fifteen-year-old peacemaker from Dorchester, Massachusetts, who was worried about violence in his community. He dreamed of becoming the first black president of the United States.
>
> Louis was the innocent victim of a gang shooting in 1993. After his death, his parents wanted to tell Louis's story. The skills we will be learning in the Peacezone program were important to Louis because he wanted all children to be safe and achieve their dreams.

STEP 2 —— **Personalize the program for the students.**

You can ask questions like these:

▶ How important is it to be safe in our school?

► How important is it for children to have dreams for the future?

► What kind of dreams do you have?

► Do you think you would like to learn more about Louis?

Tell students that Louis's story will inspire everyone to use the Peacezone skills to create peace at school, at home, and in the community.

STEP 3 —— **Introduce the next two lessons.**

Explain that you will be getting back to Louis's story soon, but that the first two lessons in the Peacezone program will be about staying safe and understanding peace.

The Right to Feel Safe

OBJECTIVE Students will identify safe and unsafe feelings and situations.

MATERIALS
- ▶ Red and green crayons or markers
- ▶ *For the first-grade extension:* Drawing paper and additional crayons or markers

VOCABULARY **cue** **right** **red flag** **green flag**

PROCEDURE

STEP 1 —— **Help students recognize when a situation is safe.**

Ask your class questions such as the following:

- ▶ Have you ever watched other kids when they're playing on the swings or riding the merry-go-round at the park or the fair?
- ▶ How do you think those kids felt?
- ▶ How could you tell they felt that way?
- ▶ What was happening around them?
- ▶ What did their faces and bodies look like?

Discuss the idea that the way that these kids look helps us to know if they feel safe or are in a safe situation. Let students know that a **right** is something every student can expect to have. One right that all students have is the right to feel safe.

STEP 2 —— **Introduce the idea of an unsafe situation.**

Ask questions such as the following:

- ▶ Have you ever watched other kids or adults who looked scared?
- ▶ How could you tell that they felt that way?

▶ What did their faces and bodies look like?

▶ What was happening around them?

Discuss the idea that the way these people look helps us to know if they feel unsafe or are in an unsafe situation.

STEP 3 —— **Define the word** *cue.*

Explain that sometimes we can know how people feel, even if they don't tell us in words:

> They tell us through cues. A **cue** about feelings is something people show us through their faces and bodies. The kids on the swings or the merry-go-round gave you cues to show you that they were happy and in a safe situation. The adults and children who looked scared gave you cues so that you knew how they felt and that they were in an unsafe situation.

Ask students what their faces and bodies would look like if they felt happy and safe. What would their faces and bodies look like if they felt unhappy and unsafe?

STEP 4 —— **Introduce the topic of red flags and green flags.**

Discuss the following ideas:

> We have special names for the ways people show us when they are in safe and unsafe situations. When people give us cues that tell us that they are feeling unsafe and scared, we call these cues **red flags.**

> When people give us cues that tell us they are feeling safe and happy, we call those cues **green flags.**

STEP 5 —— **Explain how to use red and green flags to help others.**

Discuss with students how we can look for red and green flags to make sure that others are feeling safe. Tell them that first, however, they have to make sure that they are safe. It's important to remember that we can't help anyone else unless we ourselves are safe.

You can give students the following example:

> If a child is stuck on top of a jungle gym and is giving off red flags, you must make sure that you are safe before helping that child. Instead of climbing up to help and getting stuck, too, you can find an adult who will help that child down.

STEP 6 —— **Do the Safe and Unsafe Situations activity.**

Have students turn to page 2 in their Student Manuals (Safe and Unsafe Situations). Encourage the students to color each flag on the page either red or green, depending on whether they think the students depicted feel safe.

When they have finished, briefly discuss their responses.

First-grade extension: On a separate piece of paper, have students draw a picture of a time they felt safe.

STEP 7 —— **Apply the idea of red and green flags to students' own lives.**

Ask questions such as the following:

▶ Have any of you ever felt that something good was going to happen? *(green flag)* What did that feel like?

▶ Where in your body did you feel different from the way you normally do?

▶ Have any of you ever felt that something bad was going to happen? *(red flag)* What did that feel like?

▶ Where in your body did you feel different from the way you normally do?

Repeat the idea that sometimes our own bodies give us cues that will tell us whether we are in a safe or unsafe situation. Let students know that if they feel they are in an unsafe situation, they can find an adult they know who can help them.

LESSON 2

What Is Peace?

OBJECTIVE
Students will define the word *peace* and become familiar with other peaceful and peace-related terms and symbols.

MATERIALS
▶ Crayons or markers

▶ *For the first-grade extension:* Copies of the Peace Ribbon activity (page 21)

VOCABULARY
peace

PROCEDURE

STEP 1 —— **Define the word *peace*.**

Explain that **peace** means working together and getting along instead of fighting. In the Peacezone program, students are learning skills so they can create peace.

STEP 2 —— **Discuss what peaceful situations and situations that are not peaceful feel like.**

Ask students to recall the red and green flags that you discussed in Lesson 1 and to think of the way they feel when they are in a green-flag situation: When they are in a situation and are giving off green flags, they are in a peaceful situation.

Ask questions about green-flag situations. For example:

▶ How do you feel when you are in a peaceful situation?

▶ Why do you feel this way? (Is it quiet? Is it the way people are treating one another?)

▶ Where are some peaceful places you've been?

Ask questions about red-flag situations. For example:

▶ How do you feel when you are in a situation that is not peaceful?

▶ Why do you feel this way? (What are people saying? Is there a lot of noise? How do people treat one another?)

Discuss with students whether they would rather be in a peaceful situation *(green flag)* or a situation that is not peaceful *(red flag).*

STEP 3 —— **Identify ways to create peace.**

Ask students to give examples of times at school or at home when they made peace with someone or helped someone solve a problem peacefully. For example, they may have shared TV time with a sibling or taken turns on the playground.

Identify ways to make the school more peaceful. As a class, brainstorm different ways that you can make the school more peaceful— for instance, talking over a problem instead of yelling, or waiting quietly at the drinking fountain instead of pushing.

STEP 4 —— **Do the Signs of Peace activity.**

Have students turn to page 3 of their Student Manuals (Signs of Peace). Explain that the pictures are different signs that mean peace.

Referring to these signs, first have students practice giving the peace sign with their fingers and explain that this gesture means peace. Next explain that a purple ribbon means peace and have students color the ribbon purple. (Explain that the ribbon is upside down so it will resemble the peace sign that students make with their fingers.) Finally, explain how the peace sign also means peace. Have students color the peace sign however they wish.

First-grade extension: Give each student a copy of the Peace Ribbon activity. Have students color the ribbon purple, then cut the ribbon out and give it to a person they feel creates peace at home, in school, or in the community.

STEP 5 —— **Explain the difference between peaceful and violent words and phrases.**

Discuss how we use words to tell people what we think and how we feel:

Some words we use can make people feel good and safe. These are peaceful words. Some words we use can make people feel sad and unsafe. These are violent words. We should try our best to use peaceful words.

As a class, brainstorm a list of peaceful words and phrases. Sample responses include *please and thank you, excuse me,* and *you're welcome.*

Next ask students to think of words and phrases that are violent. Then ask them to think of alternative peaceful words. For example, *move* versus *excuse me,* or *I hate you* versus *I'm angry.*

If you have students who speak different languages at home, you can have them tell you how to say peace in these languages. Recite these words for peace together as a class.

PEACEZONE

Peace Ribbon

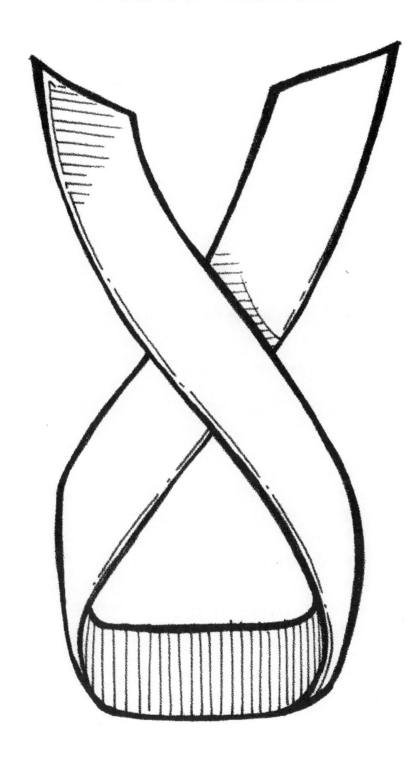

Louis D. Brown Story

OBJECTIVE Students will learn more about the life of Louis D. Brown and identify the feelings of grief and worry.

MATERIALS
- ▶ *For the Sad Sally Box:* A copy of the Sad Sally illustration (page 30), a medium-sized box, glue, and any decorations you wish
- ▶ Copies of the I-Can't Worry activity (page 31)
- ▶ Crayons or markers
- ▶ Louis D. Brown Home Page (Appendix D)
- ▶ *For the first-grade extension:* Paper and pencils

VOCABULARY **grief**   **worry**

PROCEDURE *Before teaching this lesson, make a Sad Sally box for your classroom by photocopying the illustration, gluing it to the box, and decorating the box if you wish. Please also take the time to read the adult version of the Louis D. Brown Story (in Appendix B).*

STEP 1 —— **Read and discuss Louis's story.**

Read the student version of the Louis D. Brown Story aloud to your class. (This version appears at the end of this lesson and on pages 4–7 in the Student Manual.)

STEP 2 —— **Discuss the story with your class.**

Ask questions such as the following:

- ▶ What kind of a person was Louis D. Brown? *(kind, peaceful, honest, a good student)*
- ▶ How did Louis act toward other people? Did he help people? If so, how?

► Did Louis have a positive attitude? If so, how do you know? *(his actions, things he said)*

► How do you think Louis's family felt when he died?

Discuss the idea that sometimes bad things happen, even if we act peacefully. A bad thing happened to Louis. But if we try to be peaceful and have peaceful friends, bad things are a lot less likely to happen to us.

STEP 3 —— **Ask students to relate Louis's story to their own lives.**

Ask questions such as the following:

► Have you ever lost someone or something close to you? *(a family member who left the home after divorce, a pet who died, a friend or relative who moved away)*

► How did you feel when this happened? How did you act?

STEP 4 —— **Define the word *grief.***

Discuss how when someone we love dies or is no longer part of our lives, the very, very sad feeling we get is called **grief.**

Explain that grief can last for a long time, but there are some things we can do to help ourselves:

One thing is to remember that grief and sadness don't last forever and that with time we will start to feel better. You can think about things you did with the person and draw pictures or write stories to remember those times. You can also talk with other people about how you feel.

To help students feel less sad about Louis's death, you can tell them that Louis's parents helped to write the Peacezone program because they wanted kids everywhere to learn how to be peaceful and so what happened to Louis wouldn't happen to other children.

STEP 5 —— **Talk about different kinds of worries.**

Ask students what it means to be worried about something. Explain that if you have a **worry,** it means that you are afraid that something bad might happen.

Introduce the idea of worries that you *can* do something about. Give students an example from your own life. For instance, you might be worried about being late for work. You can do something about this worry, like setting your alarm for an earlier time or making sure that you get your clothes for the day ready the night before. Ask students to suggest other things you could do about this worry.

Next ask students for examples of these kinds of worries from their own lives and what they could do about them. Some examples include worrying about getting a bad grade on a report card *(Work harder)*, getting on the wrong bus *(Have an adult write the bus number down)*, and making friends *(Offer to share a game or toy with someone you don't know well)*.

Tell students that sometimes we have worries that we *can't* do too much about:

> For example, if someone is sick, we can try to play quietly, draw pictures to cheer the person up, or bring him or her a glass of juice to show how much we care. Unfortunately, we can't actually make the person get better.

If appropriate, give an example from your own life about a worry that you can't do anything about.

STEP 6 —— **Introduce Sad Sally.**

Introduce the character Sad Sally to the class. Hold up the Sad Sally box and explain that Sally can listen to their worries. Once Sally listens to a student's worries, she asks one question: Is this worry something the student can do something about?

Tell students that when they give the worries they can't do anything about to Sad Sally, they won't have to think about them as much and can focus on other things instead.

Give additional examples of times in which students might worry. As you describe each situation, ask the class to decide whether they can or can't do something about it. Ask students to raise their hands if they think they can.

Sample situations include the following:

▶ I worry about getting to school on time. *(can do)*

▶ I worry about my grandma because she is sick. *(can't do)*

▶ I worry that I will forget to bring my lunch to school. *(can do)*

▶ I worry about my dog because he is lost. *(can do)*

STEP 7 —— **Encourage students to identify their I-Can Worries and to give Sad Sally their I-Can't Worries.**

Have students turn to page 8 (I-Can Worry) and invite them to draw a picture of a worry they have that they *can* do something about. When they are finished, ask for volunteers to share their drawings.

Next hand out copies of the I-Can't Worry activity and invite students to draw a picture of something they *can't* do anything about. After they have finished, encourage them to come up to the front, one at a time, share their worry with the class, and give their worry to Sad Sally by putting it in the box.

> *First-grade extension: Ask students to write a letter to Sad Sally. You can provide them with a beginning: "Dear Sad Sally: Sometimes I worry about _____ ."*

STEP 8 —— **Assign the Louis D. Brown Home Page.**

Give each student a copy of the Louis D. Brown Home Page. Encourage students to take the page home and share it with their parents or caregivers.

Louis D. Brown Story

Joseph M. Chéry

Meet Louis

This is a drawing of Louis David Brown. He was fifteen years old when he died. Louis lived in Boston, Massachusetts, in a neighborhood called Dorchester.

Louis

Louis did not like to go out. He preferred to be home so he could play video games, read, and watch television. Louis spent a lot of time playing with his younger sister, Allie, and his baby brother, Allen. He loved them very much. He liked to teach them games and liked to tell them stories.

Louis loved to eat. He enjoyed rice, chicken, and beans, but his favorite was Chinese food.

Louis's parents were very protective of their children. Although Louis was a teenager, they drove him everywhere he had to go. His father drove him to the school bus stop every morning. His grandmother picked him up from the train station after school.

Dorchester, where Louis lived, is very big, and lots of people live there. There are lots of cars on the streets. Louis could not wait to turn sixteen years old; he would learn how to drive like his father.

People sometimes get very violent on the streets. Some kids carry knives or guns in their pockets or under their jackets. Louis did not like that. He thought that everybody in Dorchester and everywhere else should be friends and that they should protect one another.

Louis didn't like guns, and he didn't like knives, either. He thought that when two people disagree about something, they should not fight; instead, they should act peacefully and talk out their differences.

Dream High

One day, Louis was in his bedroom playing with his cousin Antonio and his friend Anthony. They were talking about what they wanted to be when they grew up. Louis said to them: "I am going to be the first black president of the United States when I am thirty-five years old." Antonio was so happy to hear that, he jumped off the bed where he was sitting. "Wow!" he said. "That means you will also be the youngest president ever. Fantastic, then I will be your vice president." "Good," said Louis. "I want you guys and all my friends to be with me in the White House."

One night, Louis was watching the news on television. The news anchor reported that earlier that day two young men had been arguing about drugs, and one had shot the other and killed him. Louis got very sad. He looked at his father with tears in his eyes. "Too many kids are dying on the streets," he said to his father. "Why are there so many guns around? Why do people have to use drugs? That stuff can hurt you, and it can kill you."

Louis sat silently for a moment. Then he shook his head and said to his father: "If things don't change by the time I become president, I will be alone in the White House— none of my friends will be around. They will all be in jail, all addicted to drugs, or all dead."

Be Yourself

Louis was a good student; he always had good grades. One day, his parents received a letter from the school saying that Louis was not doing his homework. His parents went to see the teacher. "We do not understand," said Louis's mother. "Every night, Louis does his homework, and we review it together. Why is it that he is not bringing it to school?"

When Louis got home, his father told him that they had met with his teacher and they knew all about the homework.

"I can't turn my homework in," Louis said, "because the students in my class said it is not cool to be smart."

"The best way to be cool," said his father, "is to be yourself. If you want to become president, you have to do what you know is right, not what the kids in school say."

"I am sorry," said Louis. "I will bring all the missing homework assignments to my teacher." From that day on, Louis always brought his homework to school.

His classmates used to joke about him and say that he was a little strange at times. But he never let it bother him. In fact, he earned the respect of his classmates by sticking to his beliefs and by continuing to do well in school, despite the comments of others.

A Guiding Light

One day, Louis was talking to his cousin Antoinette. "Louis," she said, "I joined this cool group called Teens Against Gang Violence (TAGV); you should come and check it out."

"All right," said Louis. "I will come, but I am not making any promises." "That's okay," said Antoinette. "I know you will like it because it is a group of young people who are against violence just like you. The group is also against drugs."

Louis attended a meeting of Teens Against Gang Violence and liked it. The same day, he joined the group.

A few days later, he was telling his mother about how exciting the group was. "The group is really cool," he told her. "The kids are nice, but the most important thing is that we are being trained to be mediators. A mediator is someone who educates people and helps them solve problems. We speak to other kids and even adults about the dangers of guns and drugs."

"You seem quite happy with this new group," his mother said.

"Yes, Ma," Louis replied. "I want to learn all that I can so I can help kids my age to stop this violence."

"That is very thoughtful of you," said Louis' mother. "This is truly the work of a leader, the work of a future president."

"Yes, Ma," Louis said. "I want to teach people how to make peace and live peacefully."

"You should thank Antoinette for telling you about Teens Against Gang Violence," said Louis's mother. "By leading you to this positive group, she has been a role model, a guiding light for peace. Now you can be a guiding light for others."

"Yes, Ma," Louis replied. "You are right. I will thank Antoinette for being my guiding light."

Louis continued to attend meetings of the Teens Against Gang Violence. He learned how to speak to large groups of people. Louis also learned to mediate fights, which means that when kids were fighting, he knew how to help them resolve their conflict peacefully.

Louis had big dreams. He wanted to influence and change the way his generation behaved. He wanted to be the first black president of the United States. He was helping teens stop acting violently and stop using guns. Louis had a lot of work to do, and he was ready.

But Louis never saw his dreams come true. He never finished the work he had started because the same violence he was trying to stop put an end to Louis's life. On December 20, 1993, five days before Christmas, Louis was on his way to meet with the Teens Against Gang Violence when two gangs started shouting at each other. Louis was walking by when the shooting started. He got shot and died.

Louis's parents and friends cried a lot when Louis was killed. They still cry sometimes. But Louis's parents decided that the work that Louis had started must continue. To make it happen, to stop the violence the way Louis wanted, they need your help. They need you to continue the work for Louis.

Sad Sally

Peacezone: A Program for Teaching Social Literacy—Teacher's Guide (Grades K–1)

PEACEZONE

I-Can't Worry

LESSON 4

Louis D. Brown Reading Response: Feelings

OBJECTIVE Students will identify and express their feelings as they continue to explore the life of Louis D. Brown.

MATERIALS
- ▶ Sad Sally box (from Lesson 3)
- ▶ An assortment of wooden building blocks

PROCEDURE

STEP 1 — **Review the discussion about the Louis D. Brown story.**

Ask students to tell you what they learned in the last lesson about Louis D. Brown and grief. Hold up the Sad Sally box and remind students that Sally is holding on to their worries.

STEP 2 — **Discuss what happens when people keep their feelings inside.**

Tell students that sometimes it is hard for people to talk about how they feel. Doing this can be difficult for both children and adults.

Show students the blocks and tell them you are going to build a tower. Begin building the tower as you explain that we can keep all of our feelings inside and never tell anyone how we feel. Pretty soon, our feelings build up inside of us, just like the blocks are building up.

Ask the students what will happen if you keep making the tower taller. *(It will fall or break down.)*

Let students know that if people let their feelings build up inside of them and don't tell anyone how they feel, they can feel as though they may break down, too. When they do, they might yell at people when they don't mean to yell or become very tired and not feel like doing anything.

STEP 3 —— **Practice identifying feelings.**

Tell students that sometimes practicing helps it become easier to tell people how we feel. To illustrate, ask students how they felt at different points in Louis's story—for example, *happy* when Louis said he wanted to be president or *sad* when he died.

STEP 4 —— **Do the Feelings activity.**

Continue the previous idea by asking students to turn to page 9 in their Student Manuals (Feelings). Help students choose one face/feeling and then complete the sentence by adding their own situation. Give assistance as needed.

Ask for volunteers to tell you what feeling and situation they chose. Discuss how the faces and feelings relate to the situations students describe.

STEP 5 —— **Talk about what we do with our feelings.**

Explain that feelings are not good or bad:

It is what we *do* with our feelings, how we *act,* that is good or bad. It is okay to be angry if someone else gets in front of you in line to go to lunch. It is not okay to shove that person out of the way. It is okay to ask the person to please go to the end of the line or to ask a teacher for help.

Louis D. Brown Reading Response: Goals and Dreams

OBJECTIVE

As they continue to explore the life of Louis D. Brown, students will learn how to set goals to make their dreams come true.

MATERIALS

Crayons or markers

VOCABULARY

goal   dream

PROCEDURE

STEP 1 —— **Review the discussion about feelings from the previous lesson.**

Ask students what they learned in the last lesson: Did thinking about and practicing identifying their feelings help them? If so, how?

STEP 2 —— **Discuss how Louis's family remembers him.**

Talk to students about how Louis was proud of himself for some of the things that he did. His parents and brother and sister were proud of him, too. Remembering the things Louis did or said to make them proud or to make them laugh really helped them to feel a little less sad about Louis's death.

Ask questions such as the following:

▶ What did Louis do that might have made him or his parents feel proud?

▶ What are some of the things you've done that have made you or your parents proud?

Explain that, because Louis's parents were very proud of him, they tell his story and show his picture to a lot of grown-ups and children.

STEP 3 —— **Discuss goals and dreams.**

Ask the following questions:

▶ What is a **goal?** *(A goal is something you decide you are going to do.)*

▶ What is a **dream?** *(A dream is something good you'd like to have happen to you or in your life.)*

Explain that to make your dreams come true, you need to set goals for yourself.

Discuss an example from your own life of a dream that you have had and the goals you set to reach that dream. You might say that you always dreamed of becoming a teacher, so you studied hard in school and set a goal to go to college. Emphasize that if students keep working toward their goals, they will be able to achieve their dreams.

STEP 4 —— **Relate the idea of goals and dreams to students' lives.**

Ask students what their dreams are: What is one goal they might have that would help them reach their dream? For example, if your dream is to play the piano, you might set the goals to take lessons and practice every day.

STEP 5 —— **Do the Goals and Dreams activity.**

Ask students to turn to page 10 in their Student Manuals (Goals and Dreams) and distribute the crayons or markers. Encourage students to draw a picture of a goal or dream they have.

When the students have finished, ask for volunteers to share their work.

Pledge for Peace

The Pledge for Peace is an integral tool in the establishment of a positive classroom climate. When the pledge is displayed on a poster in the classroom, it can be used as a reference throughout the day. When used in this way, the pledge gives positive reinforcement for positive behaviors. When students are exhibiting behaviors that do not follow the pledge, reminding them and referring them to the poster can be very effective in helping them self-correct their behavior.

Teachers have found that the morning time slot, immediately following circle time or morning exercises, is an effective time to recite the pledge. The pledge should not be merely recited by rote, however. Varying the ways the pledge is presented keeps it fresh. In addition to reciting the pledge, a single student may read it aloud while others read it silently. Another day, the class might sing the pledge. Use your imagination to find a variety of ways to present the pledge.

It is also important to discuss the pledge frequently with the class. Get students to think about the meaning behind the words by citing examples from your own life and asking them to think of examples from their lives. Refer to the pledge throughout the day.

When students are doing a great job respecting diversity, using peaceful words, or displaying other desirable behaviors, remind them that they are successfully using the pledge. When they need to improve in certain areas, remind them that the Pledge for Peace is a pledge we make to ourselves. It is something that we live by in our homes, schools, and communities.

Basic Guidelines for the Pledge

- ► Present the pledge every morning.
- ► Find a variety of ways to present the pledge.
- ► Refer to the pledge throughout the day.
- ► Discuss the pledge frequently.
- ► Make the pledge a part of your everyday language.

LESSON 1

Introducing the Pledge for Peace

OBJECTIVE Students will define and experience the four aspects of the Pledge for Peace.

MATERIALS
► Pledge for Peace poster (Appendix C)
► Chalkboard or easel pad
► Copies of the My Pledge for Peace Book activity (pages 43–44)
► Crayons or markers, glue, scissors

VOCABULARY **diversity**   **attitude**

PROCEDURE *Before teaching this lesson, hang the Pledge for Peace poster in a prominent location in your classroom.*

STEP 1 —— **Introduce the Pledge for Peace.**

Referring to the poster, read the Pledge for Peace aloud to the class. Leave the poster up for future reference.

Pledge for Peace
    I will treat others the way I want to be treated.
    I will respect the diversity of all people.
    I will use peaceful words.
    I will have a positive attitude.

Ask the class to say the pledge aloud with you.

STEP 2 —— **Discuss the idea of treating others the way you want to be treated.**

Ask students how they want their friends, classmates, or family members to treat them. You can ask questions like the following:

> ► If we had a new student in class, how should we treat that student?

> ► If you were a new student, how would you like to be treated?

STEP 3 **Discuss the concept of diversity.**

Explain that the word **diversity** means different. Let students know that they can remember this fact because *diversity* begins with the letter *d* and *different* begins with the letter *d*. Ask students to repeat the phrase "Diversity means different" with you.

Discuss how diversity means that we have things that make us special and not exactly the same as our friends or even other people in our family. Emphasize that these things are not just possessions, but the way we look, the things we like and dislike, and the beliefs we have.

You can ask the following questions:

> ► How are you different from the person sitting next to you?

> ► How are you the same?

You can also pose the following question, and variations of it, to the class: If the person sitting next to you has brown eyes and you have green eyes, should it matter?

Focus on how differences make us special and give us an opportunity to learn from one another.

STEP 4 **Discuss the use of peaceful words and phrases.**

Discuss some peaceful words we use to show people that we respect them and want to get along with them—for example, *please, thank you, would you mind,* and *sorry.*

Discuss other peaceful words that people use, like *love, share,* and *peace.* If the word has a symbol, draw the symbol and write the word next to it. (For example, you can draw a heart next to the word *love* or a peace sign next to the word *peace.*)

STEP 5 **Discuss what the word *attitude* means.**

Let students know that the word **attitude** means showing how we feel through our actions, both in the words we use and with our bodies. Having a positive attitude means acting in a polite, pleasant way.

Next ask for volunteers to come up to act attitudes out silently. Choose a volunteer and whisper to that student whether he or she should have a positive attitude or a negative attitude toward a typical situation at home or at school. For example:

▶ Your dad said you have to take out the garbage.

▶ Your teacher asked you to be quiet.

▶ Your friend lost your book.

After a student acts out the attitude, ask the rest of the class if the person showed a positive attitude or a negative attitude and how they could tell. *(facial expression, body language, and so forth)*

To judge students' comprehension, at this point you can ask them to tell you what the word *attitude* means.

STEP 6 —— **Share an example of a way you use the Pledge for Peace.**

Share ways you, as an adult, use the Pledge for Peace. For example, you might say that you respect diversity when you meet someone who looks or sounds different from you.

STEP 7 —— **Give examples of ways students use the Pledge for Peace at home, at school, and in the community.**

Explain that the pledge is important in many situations. For example:

Home: Listening to a parent saying it is time for bed *(having a positive attitude)*

School: Waiting for another student to finish talking before you speak *(treating others the way you want to be treated)*; choosing a team for a relay race *(respecting diversity)*

Community: Asking someone to sit down in the movie theater *(using peaceful words)*

Ask students to give you additional examples of ways they use the Pledge for Peace.

STEP 8 —— **Do the My Pledge for Peace Book activity.**

Have students turn to page 12 in their Student Manuals (My Pledge for Peace) and briefly review the four aspects of the pledge.

Next give each student a copy of the My Pledge for Peace Book activity and distribute the crayons or markers, glue, and scissors.

Explain that the students will be making a book of the Pledge for Peace that they can keep or share with parents or caregivers.

Ask students to draw a picture of themselves for the first page and to color the other pictures as they wish. Give help as students need it to cut, fold, and glue their books together.

My Pledge for Peace Book

I will respect the diversity of all people.

Whether we are the same or different on the outside, it's the person we are on the inside that counts.

I will treat others the way I want to be treated.

Caring about others makes me and those around me feel good. Pushing, fighting, bullying, name-calling, and treating others badly hurts them and me.

fold on dotted line →

cut on solid line →

My Pledge for Peace Book

Name

My Pledge for Peace Book *(continued)*

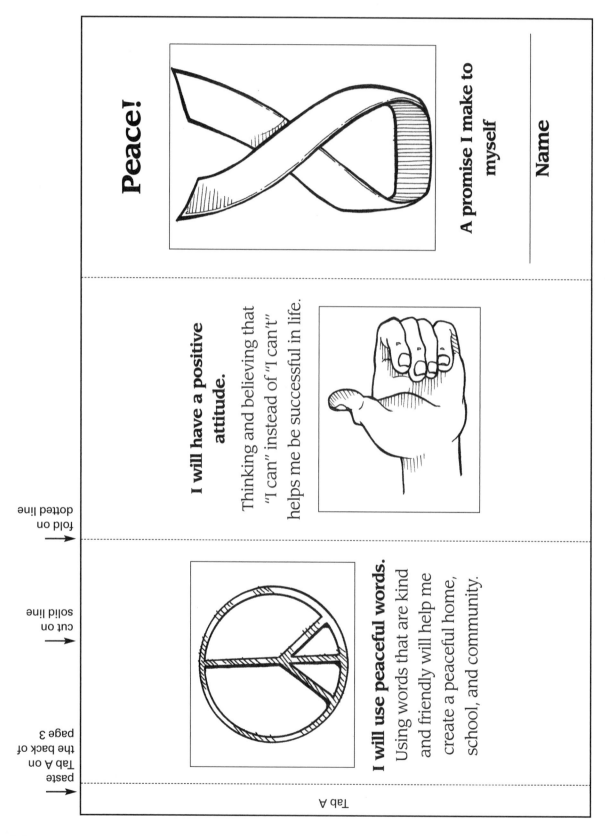

Peace!

A promise I make to myself

Name _____

I will have a positive attitude.

Thinking and believing that "I can" instead of "I can't" helps me be successful in life.

fold on dotted line

cut on solid line

paste Tab A on the back of page 3

I will use peaceful words. Using words that are kind and friendly will help me create a peaceful home, school, and community.

Tab A

LESSON 2

Living by the Pledge for Peace: Part 1

OBJECTIVE　　Students will further explore the first two aspects of the Pledge for Peace and will apply these aspects to their own lives.

MATERIALS
- ▶ Crayons or markers
- ▶ Copies of the How I Treat Others activity (page 47)

PROCEDURE

STEP 1 —— **Review the concept of treating others the way you want to be treated.**

Referring to the poster of the Pledge for Peace, point out this part of the pledge and give an example from your own life, if you wish. Encourage students to share situations from their own lives.

STEP 2 —— **Do the How I Treat Others activity.**

Have students turn to page 13 in their Student Manuals (How I Treat Others) and distribute the crayons or markers. Discuss each situation depicted and allow students to make their own judgments as to whether or not the pledge is being followed. Discuss their responses.

Next give each student a copy of the How I Treat Others activity page. Help the students generate ideas about what they can draw to illustrate the idea of treating others as they would like to be treated, then give them time to draw.

After students have finished drawing, ask for volunteers to share their drawings with the class. Post the drawings on a classroom wall or bulletin board, if you like.

First-grade extension: Help students write a caption for their picture.

STEP 3 — **Review the concept of diversity.**

Review your discussion from the previous lesson about diversity and the importance of celebrating diversity by accepting people for who they are on the inside, not on the outside. Explain that diversity means that you respect the fact that different people like different things. Talk to the students about what they like to do (hobbies, sports, TV shows, and the like) and emphasize how these kinds of differences make life interesting.

STEP 4 — **Do the Diversity of All People activity.**

Have students turn to page 14 in their Student Manuals (Diversity of All People). Ask students to color the picture.

After they have finished, discuss how the people in the picture are all different: Are they of different age groups, cultures, and so forth?

STEP 5 — **Celebrate diversity.**

Tell students they can celebrate diversity in a number of ways. For example:

► You celebrate diversity when you decide to sit next to someone at lunch, even though that person is eating a food that you don't like or have never tried before.

► You celebrate diversity when you don't make fun of someone who dresses differently because he or she has a different culture or beliefs.

First-grade extension: Have a few students volunteer to share the ways they celebrate diversity.

PEACEZONE

How I Treat Others

Living by the Pledge for Peace: Part 2

OBJECTIVE
: Students will further explore the final two aspects of the Pledge for Peace and apply these aspects to their own lives.

MATERIALS
: ▶ Crayons or markers

PROCEDURE

STEP 1 —— **Review the concept of peaceful words.**

Referring to the Pledge for Peace poster, review the idea that some words have peaceful meanings and some do not.

STEP 2 —— **Do the Peaceful Words activity.**

Ask students to turn to page 15 in their Student Manuals (Peaceful Words). Invite students to share where, when, and with whom they could use each of these words or phrases. For example, when you're playing ball outside during recess, you could tell your friend, "Good job!" when he or she scores a point.

Ask students why they think using these words can help create peace in and out of the classroom.

As a class, brainstorm other peaceful words or sayings.

STEP 3 —— **Review the concept of a positive attitude.**

Review this concept by discussing an instance in the past few days when a student exhibited a positive attitude. For example, a student might not have been feeling well yet participated in class until his or her parent arrived.

—— **Do the Thumbs-Up for a Positive Attitude activity.**

Have students turn to page 16 in their Student Manuals (Thumbs-Up for a Positive Attitude). Explain that when something is thumbs-up, that means it's good or okay; when something is thumbs-down, that means it's bad or not okay.

Discuss each situation and have students circle either thumbs-up or thumbs-down, depending on whether the attitude depicted is positive or negative.

Distribute the crayons or markers and have students color the positive-attitude picture. Finish by having a discussion of other ways children and adults can have positive attitudes in and out of school.

First-grade extension: Refer to the recess example on page 16 in the Student Manual and have students come up with ways they might show a positive attitude in the situation.

Pledge for Peace Role Model

OBJECTIVE Students will identify the qualities that make Louis D. Brown a role model for the Pledge for Peace, then will identify these qualities in people from home, school, or community.

MATERIALS
- ▶ Crayons or markers
- ▶ Drawing paper
- ▶ Copies of the Pledge for Peace Home Page (Appendix D)

VOCABULARY **role model**

PROCEDURE

STEP 1 —— **Discuss what it means to be a role model.**

Have students turn to page 17 in their Student Manuals (Pledge for Peace Role Model). Discuss the idea that being a **role model** means setting a good example for the people around you. Explain that a role model can be anyone who sets a good example at home, at school, or in the community.

STEP 2 —— **Relate the Pledge for Peace to Louis's story.**

Ask questions like the following:

- ▶ How did Louis D. Brown live by the Pledge for Peace? *(for example, by being kind to others, working with other kids to help end violence, caring about his family)*
- ▶ How we can learn from Louis and how he lived?

STEP **3** —— **Discuss how other people can also be role models for the Pledge for Peace.**

Brainstorm a list of people in the community who use the Pledge for Peace in their lives. *(for example, teachers, police, firefighters, coaches, religious leaders, and mentors)*

STEP **4** —— **Have the students make role-model posters.**

Discuss and have each student choose someone who could be a role model for the Pledge for Peace because he or she uses different parts of the pledge in daily life.

Distribute the drawing paper and crayons or markers and encourage students to create posters of the role models they chose.

When the students are finished drawing, ask for volunteers to present their drawings to the class. If you wish, display the drawings in the classroom or a public area of the school.

STEP **5** —— **Assign the Pledge for Peace Home Page.**

Give students a copy of the Pledge for Peace Home Page to take home and share with their parents or caregivers.

Trying Your Best

One of the characteristics of successful people is their ability to bounce back in difficult situations. We can never promise a child a problem-free environment; however, we can teach a child how to continue when things are hard and how to keep trying despite the many challenges that can get in the way. If children can be taught to try their best at all times, believing in themselves even when they make mistakes, they will be able to build many other skills in life. As we begin this unit, we can remind students that it is okay to make mistakes. Making mistakes is how we all learn.

As students participate in classroom activities throughout the day, reinforce the concept of trying your best and accepting mistakes as a normal part of learning. Some examples of times students could be urged to try their best include the following:

- ▶ Learning new spelling words
- ▶ Memorizing lines for a play or presentation
- ▶ Playing a game during recess
- ▶ Writing in a journal

Daily Guidelines for Trying Your Best

- ▶ Refer to the skill throughout the day as you see students working hard at a task.
- ▶ Remind students that it is okay to make mistakes. Making mistakes is how we learn.
- ▶ Discuss how both adults and children need to try their best and learn from their mistakes.
- ▶ Remind students to fill themselves with self-confidence when they try their best.

Introducing Trying Your Best

OBJECTIVE Students will define and experience the skill of Trying Your Best.

MATERIALS
- ► Trying Your Best poster (Appendix C)
- ► Crayons or markers
- ► *For the Drumroll Shake game:* A drum (or another instrument)

VOCABULARY **self-confidence**

PROCEDURE *Before teaching this lesson, hang the Trying Your Best poster in a prominent location in your classroom. Leave the poster up for future reference.*

STEP 1 — **Introduce the skill of Trying Your Best.**

Referring to the poster, read the parts of the Trying Your Best skill aloud to the class.

Trying Your Best

I will try my best.

Even when I make mistakes, I learn from them.

The most important thing is to keep trying.

When I try my best, I get a proud, happy feeling called self-confidence.

STEP 2 — **Share a story about how you, as an adult, try your best in your life.**

Tell students about a time you made a mistake and what you learned from it. For example, you might say that you forgot to get some things at the store and learned that next time you should bring a list.

STEP 3 ── **Give examples of ways students can use the skill of Trying Your Best at home, at school, and in the community.**

Share examples like the following:

> *Home:* Forgetting to do a chore, accidentally breaking a brother's or sister's toy

> *School:* Getting a spelling word wrong, forgetting to hang up your coat

> *Community:* Missing a free throw in a basketball game, forgetting to pick up your trash in the park

Have students come up with additional examples of trying their best in their own lives. They can also give examples of what they have learned from these mistakes. For instance, if a student gets a spelling word wrong, he or she would probably remember the correct spelling the next time.

STEP 4 ── **Discuss the fact that it is okay to make mistakes.**

Ask students questions like the following:

▶ What do you need to do to learn how to tie your shoes? *(practice)*

▶ What should you do if you make a mistake when tying your shoes? Should you give up or keep trying your best?

▶ What would happen if everyone gave up the first time he or she made a mistake? *(No one would learn anything.)*

STEP 5 ── **Introduce the topic of self-confidence.**

Discuss the following ideas:

▶ Trying your best gives you a proud, happy feeling called **self-confidence.**

▶ It is up to you to be proud of yourself and feel self-confident when you have tried your best. So, who can give you self-confidence? *(yourself)*

▶ You can take a deep breath and fill yourself with self-confidence. Even if you breathe out, the self-confidence stays inside you!

STEP 6 ── **Discuss examples of self-confidence.**

Ask students what companies want when they make commercials about shoes, toys, or cars: Do they want to give us self-confidence, or do they want our money? *(our money)*

Point out that self-confidence isn't something that you can get from your clothes, your toys, or the other things you own:

> It is up to us to remind ourselves that these things don't give us self-confidence. What happens when the shoes go out of style, the toys break, or the car stops running? The only person who can give you self-confidence is yourself. You get it from following the Pledge for Peace and trying your best.

If you wish, give an example of something that you feel self-confident about.

Ask students what things they feel self-confident about. Students may volunteer that they feel confident about playing an instrument or being the line leader.

If there are any characters who show self-confidence in books your class might be reading, discuss how they do so.

STEP 7 —— **Have students experience the skill of Trying Your Best by playing the following game.**

Drumroll Shake

Purpose of the game

In this game, the class will explore the skill of Trying Your Best by shaking their hands only when they hear the sound of a drum (or another instrument). Students will understand that it is okay to make mistakes as long as they are trying their best and that learning from their mistakes is important.

How to play

The object of the game is for students to shake their hands when they hear the sound of the drum. The challenge is for the students to keep their hands still when you do not hit the drum.

First, show students the drum and let them hear the sound that the instrument makes. Next, ask them to hold up their hands with their palms facing forward. Then hit the drum as the students follow by shaking their hands.

Allow students to explore the feeling of making mistakes by making it appear as if you are going to hit the drum, then stopping at the last second. Continue to reinforce the idea that they are trying their best and that it is okay to make mistakes.

After the game is over, ask students what they should do if they make a mistake. Continue discussion about why it is okay to make mistakes and how you can learn from making mistakes.

STEP 8 —— **Do the I Will Try My Best activity.**

Have the students turn to page 20 in their Student Manuals (I Will Try My Best) and distribute the crayons or markers. Have students color the pictures. As they color, talk with them about the mistakes that the characters in these pictures are making and what the characters can learn.

When students have finished coloring, ask for volunteers to tell a story about a time they made a mistake and what they learned from it.

First-grade extension: Have students write some words at the bottom of the page to describe a time they made a mistake and what they learned from it. (Give assistance as needed.)

Reinforcing Trying Your Best

OBJECTIVE Students will further explore the skill of Trying Your Best and apply it to their lives.

MATERIALS
- ▶ Crayons or markers
- ▶ Copies of the Mighty Me! activity (page 62)
- ▶ *For the first-grade extension:* Paper and pencils

PROCEDURE *After teaching this lesson, you may want to have the class nominate a Mighty Me on a daily or weekly basis. Students can nominate those they see trying their best. If you do this, it is important to find the positive in every student and to make sure everyone is designated as a Mighty Me at least once.*

STEP 1 —— **Review what the class learned in the previous lesson about the skill of Trying Your Best.**

Referring to the Trying Your Best poster, review the skill. Remind students that this skill is one that everyone, both children and adults, can use.

Ask students to tell you what they learned from the Drumroll Shake game.

STEP 2 —— **Reinforce the skill of Trying Your Best by playing the following game.**

Head, Shoulders, Knees, and Toes

Purpose of the game

Through this fun and simple game, students will strengthen the understanding that it is okay to make mistakes as long as they try their best.

How to play

Have students stand up, facing you. Explain that the purpose of the game is for students to try their best to follow you as you touch your head, shoulders, knees, or toes.

Begin the game by touching your head and saying "head." Make sure students follow and touch their heads. Let students know that they are doing a great job and should be proud because they are trying their best.

Continue the game at a slow pace by touching your shoulders, knees, and toes, each time naming the body part. Make sure that you are watching the students and reminding them that it's okay if they make a mistake.

After the students have followed these movements, make the game more challenging by switching the order of the movements. For example, you can move from your head to your toes, to your knees, and back to your toes. You can even say the name of one body part while touching another.

The main message to convey is that it is okay to make mistakes, but you can also reinforce the idea that trying their best helps students be successful, even if initially they do not succeed.

After the game is over, you can ask the following questions:

▶ Did you give up, or did you keep trying your best during the game? Did anyone feel like giving up? What could happen if you gave up?

▶ Is it okay to make mistakes?

▶ If someone makes a mistake, should you make fun of the person and laugh?

▶ How would the person who made a mistake feel if you made fun of him or her?

▶ How could you help a person who has made a mistake feel better? *(by encouraging him or her and saying nice things)*

▶ What are some other times when you have to try your best in school? When do you try your best at home or in the neighborhood?

STEP 3 —— **Introduce the idea of a Mighty Me.**

Have students turn to page 21 in their Student Manuals and explain that when they are feeling sad or mad, they can pretend that they have a "Mighty Me" inside them:

Your Mighty Me can help you when you feel mad or sad because it can remind you to try your best without giving up. Your Mighty Me keeps trying, even if you make a mistake.

Ask the students for examples of times their Mighty Me could help them when they are feeling sad or mad—for example, when they have been told they can't do something they want very much to do.

If you wish, give an example from your life of how your Mighty Me helps you when you're feeling sad or mad.

STEP 4 —— **Do the Mighty Me! activity.**

Give each student a copy of the Mighty Me! activity. Distribute the crayons or markers and invite students to draw a picture of what their own Mighty Me looks like.

When students have finished drawing, ask for volunteers to share their drawings with the class. If you wish, post the pictures on a classroom wall or bulletin board.

First-grade extension: On a separate piece of paper, students can create a comic strip featuring their Mighty Me.

Mighty Me!

LESSON 3

Learning through Literature: Trying Your Best Stories

OBJECTIVE — Students will relate what they have learned about the skill of Trying Your Best to a story from the life of Louis D. Brown.

MATERIALS
- ▶ Copies of the Trying Your Best Home Page (Appendix D)
- ▶ *Optional:* A copy of the story you choose to read to the class for each student to keep or take home

PROCEDURE

STEP 1 — **Read the story best suited to your class.**

Myesha's First Friend

—Recommended for kindergarten

Synopsis: Myesha doesn't enjoy her first day of school because she is shy and scared to make friends. When she comes home crying, her cousin Jermaine tells her she's a wonderful person and that if she just tries her best to get to know people, they will want to be friends with her. The next day, even though she is very scared, she follows her cousin's advice and starts talking to Louis, the boy who sits next to her. That's when Myesha realizes that her cousin was right all along.

Read the story on pages 66–67.

After you have finished reading the story, discuss how the story relates to the skill of Trying Your Best. You can ask the following questions:

- ▶ In the beginning of the story, Myesha says none of the kids liked her the first day of school. Do you think that's true, or do you think they didn't speak to her because she didn't speak to them first?

▶ When Myesha tells Jermaine why she's sad, he tells her that as long as she is herself and tries her best, everything will be fine. Is it ever right to try to be someone else in order to make friends?

▶ At the end of the story, Myesha uses her self-confidence and opens up to people and gets over her fears. What was your first day of school like? How did you try your best and use your self-confidence to make friends?

The New Bicycle

—Recommended for first grade

Synopsis: Louis dreams of a new bike. When he gets it, he is excited and can't wait to ride it. Unfortunately, he has a hard time learning how to steer his bike and is embarrassed in front of all his friends when he falls down. Despite falling down, he gets back up and tries his best to master riding his new bicycle.

Read the story on pages 68–69.

After the story is over, discuss how it relates to the skill of Trying Your Best. You can ask the following questions:

▶ What was Louis's problem at the beginning of the story?

▶ How do you think Louis felt when he kept falling off his bike?

▶ What did Louis's friends do to help him out? How do you think Louis would have felt if his friends had laughed at him or called him names?

▶ Did Louis give up when learning to ride his bike? How do you think this made him feel?

▶ What would have happened if Louis got so angry and upset that he didn't keep getting back on his bike? What do you think Louis would do the next time he tried to do something hard?

▶ Was there ever a time when you didn't know how to do something? Did you try your best? What did you do?

STEP 2 —— **Discuss the Trying Your Best Role Model.**

Have the class turn to page 22 in their Student Manuals (Trying Your Best Role Model). Remind students that a role model is someone who sets a good example for other people.

You can ask students the following questions:

- ► How does the police officer use the skill of Trying Your Best?
- ► Is the police officer a good role model for this skill?
- ► How are other people in the community good role models for this skill?

STEP 3 —— **Assign the Trying Your Best Home Page.**

Give students a copy of the Trying Your Best Home Page to share with their parents or caregivers.

Myesha's First Friend

Blue Telusma

After my first day of kindergarten, I felt like crying. It was the worst day. As soon as Mom dropped me off at the school, I got scared, and because I was so shy, I didn't talk to anyone all day.

When I got back to my house after school, I couldn't stop worrying about what the next day would be like. I kept wondering what would happen if I never made any friends. Or what if nobody liked me? I thought that would be the worst.

As I played with my dolls in my bedroom and thought about the next day, my cousin Jermaine stepped into my room and said, "Hey, kiddo! How was your first day of school?"

"Horrible," I sighed, fixing my doll's hair. "I think my dolls are going to be my only friends."

"Don't be silly. I know how much you like playing with your dolls, but don't you want real friends who can talk to you? Did something happen at school?"

"None of the kids like me," I cried.

"Aw, why do you say that?" Jermaine said, pulling me into his arms.

"Because nobody talked to me all day!"

"Well, did you try to talk to anyone first?"

"No."

"See, that's your problem, Myesha," Jermaine said. "You need to let them see what a cool person you are. Tomorrow when you go to school, introduce yourself to at least one person, and just be yourself. I bet once the kids get to know you, you'll have plenty of friends."

"Really? You think so?" I asked, getting excited about his idea.

"I know so," he said, giving me a hug. "As long as you try your best to get to know the other kids."

Myesha's First Friend *(continued)*

The next day, I spent the whole morning working up the nerve to go talk to someone. Finally, during recess I spotted a little boy sitting alone on the swings, watching the other kids play. He looked as lonely as I did, so I figured it would be safe to go up to him.

"Hi, my name is Myesha," I said, sitting down on the swing next to him.

The little boy looked up at me with a surprised look on his face. "Hey, I'm Louis," he said, smiling. "You want to play with this ball?"

"Um . . . okay!" I said, getting up to follow him.

I never really played much with balls, but Louis said it was no problem. And I was so happy to have a new friend that I didn't really care what we played.

The next day I sat next to Louis in class, and we shared crayons during art class. As time went by, I started to talk to the other kids in class, too.

Getting over my shyness was hard, but every day I tried my best not to be afraid and to talk to other people. By the time Halloween came, I had tons of friends to play with at school.

My cousin was right. All I had to do was be myself and try my best. Now I love school!

PEACEZONE

The New Bicycle

Joseph M. Chéry

Day and night, when he was walking to school and when he was at home watching television, Louis thought about it. It was a bike. He wanted a bicycle so badly. He begged his father every night before he went to sleep to buy him a bicycle. Every night, his father said that bicycles were very expensive and that they couldn't afford one. So every week, Louis set aside fifty cents toward his bike in an old shoebox with the word *bike* written on it in green crayon.

When school ended in June, Louis gave all of the money he had saved to his father, but he knew it still wasn't enough for a bike. His dad looked as though he was going to cry that night, but then he tucked the covers around Louis and said, "We'll see."

Louis sat looking out the window, watching his friends whoosh right by him on their bicycles—a bright red bicycle with a horn, a yellow one with black lightning bolts. Louis wanted to have fun riding down the street, zooming past his friends, feeling the wind whistling in his ears as he pedaled down the street.

That July, Louis's dream came true. He woke up one morning, and there was a brand new blue and black bicycle with a red ribbon on it waiting in the kitchen! It was a two-wheel bicycle—the kind all of the big kids had. Louis was so excited! He didn't know how to ride a two-wheeler, but he started right out the door to show his friends. He opened the door, and he heard his father calling his name. Louis thought about pretending that he had not heard his dad, but then he remembered that his father had, after all, bought him the new bicycle. He stopped.

"Louis," said his father, "come back and get your helmet and elbow and knee pads! You don't want to hurt yourself—then you won't be able to ride your bike anywhere!"

Louis put the helmet and elbow and knee pads on and started outside again. His friends were already on the street playing and riding their bicycles. When they saw Louis with his new bike, they all gathered around him to look at it and touch it.

"It's beautiful," one of them said.

"Yes, it is," Louis replied proudly.

The New Bicycle *(continued)*

"Do you need some help learning to ride your two-wheeler?" another friend asked.

"That's okay. I'm going to ride my new bike all by myself!" Louis replied as he sat on the shiny black and blue seat and started pedaling. For one magic moment, Louis was sailing down the street. Then the bike started wiggling from side to side, and the front wheel started turning as though it had a mind of its own. He tried to keep pedaling, but Louis and the bike were soon wrapped together on the ground.

Some of his friends giggled. Others encouraged him, "Come on, get up, you can do it!"

Louis looked at his arms and legs—no cuts, thanks to the pads that his dad had given him. He stomped past his friends and straightened the bike up again.

Again, he started pedaling as fast as he could, and again Louis and his blue and black bicycle wound up on the ground. Louis looked at his friends. "Oh, no!" he thought. More of them gathered around to watch him. Louis thought to himself, "You can do it! Just try your best!" Again, he picked up his bike, dusted off his jeans, and climbed back on.

"You go, Louis! You can do it!" someone yelled. Louis started pedaling again. The bike wiggled, but Louis kept holding onto the handlebars and made sure the bike went straight ahead. Soon he could really feel the wind blowing in his ears and heard his friends cheering for him. Still, he just thought about pedaling and balancing himself on the bike.

Soon Louis had pedaled down the entire block! He stopped the bike, out of breath, but started laughing because he was so happy. His friends ran over to him. "Pretty good, for a first time! We are so proud of you," they said.

Louis was so happy he hadn't given up on trying to ride his bike. He kept trying his best, even after he fell, until he could ride by himself. As a matter of fact, when he thought about it, he was proud of himself! He couldn't wait to get home and tell his dad!

Community Service Learning: Peaceful Neighborhood

OBJECTIVE   Students will learn about the concepts of community and community service and will apply the skill of Trying Your Best as they complete a community service project.

MATERIALS   ▶ Blocks (Legos or Duplos), Playmobil figures, additional props and materials as desired

VOCABULARY   **community**   **community service**

PROCEDURE

STEP 1 —— **Discuss the definition of *community.***

Explain that a **community** is a group of people who live or work together:

> A community is not just the neighborhood in which people live. Any group of people with something in common and the place they live, work, or play form a community.

> Schools can be communities, and classrooms can be communities, too, because both of these places are made up of people who work together. Neighborhoods and cities are also communities for that same reason.

Ask students:

▶ Do all communities look the same?

▶ What do the members of different communities have in common? *(They are people who work together.)*

STEP 2 —— **Define and discuss *community service.***

Discuss ideas such as the following:

Every community needs its residents to invest a little time, a little energy, and a little care in helping to keep the community beautiful, safe, and healthy. Each of us, no matter how young or how old we may be, can give to our community.

The things we give to our community are known as **community service.** Community service can be a lot of different things. Community service can be anything from cleaning up a messy playground to picking up a pencil when someone drops it.

Community service can be something very simple, something that makes you feel good inside when you do it. It can be something that benefits one person, or it can benefit everyone in the community.

Community service shows that you care for both the people and the community. We can learn from community service as we do it.

STEP 3 —— **Relate the Pledge for Peace and the skill of Trying Your Best to the idea of community service.**

Referring to the Pledge for Peace Poster, repeat how important it is to treat others the way you want to be treated, respect diversity in others, use peaceful words, and have a positive attitude:

> When we do this, we have to remember that it's okay to make mistakes as long as we keep trying. As we do our community service activities, we always need to try to use the Pledge for Peace.

STEP 4 —— **Introduce the project.**

Explain that students will be building a peaceful neighborhood from the materials you have collected.

Discuss how the classroom community is improving because of the project, what makes the neighborhood they're building a community, and how important it is to try their best as they work on the project.

STEP 5 —— **Do the project.**

Using the materials collected, have students build the peaceful neighborhood in a designated area of the classroom.

You can ask students questions such as the following:

▶ What community will they be helping by building the peaceful neighborhood?

▶ How is this neighborhood a community?

- How will you make the peaceful neighborhood safe?
- How will the people in this community act toward one another?
- Will there be people whose job it is to help bring peace? *(police officers, peer mediators, parents, judges, and so forth)*
- What will you do if you make a mistake while working on building the neighborhood?
- What parts of the Pledge for Peace will you need to use as you work on the project?
- Why will you need them?

STEP 6 —— **Present the project.**

The neighborhood can be an ongoing part of the students' classroom experience. Update the project with additional people, buildings, and so on, throughout the remainder of the school year.

If possible, invite police and fire department and other public service personnel into the classroom to discuss how they try their best to keep the community safe.

STEP 7 —— **Take time to reflect.**

Discuss the changes and improvements in the peaceful neighborhood periodically. You can ask the following questions:

General questions

- What was doing this project like for you?
- Which part of the project did you like the least? The most?
- What parts of the Pledge for Peace did you use while you were doing this project?

Specific questions

- How do you feel about our peaceful neighborhood?
- How is the neighborhood helping us out as a class?
- What do you think our neighborhood needs to make it even better?

Self-Control

Throughout our lives, we must all exercise self-control to resist temptation, to follow directions, and, ultimately, to stay safe and be successful. In the past, we may have expected children to use their self-control without understanding what it is. We are now learning that we have to teach students what self-control is and ways to control themselves throughout their lives. Through self-control, children discover that they are in charge of what they do and what they say.

Why should we use self-control? Self-control is a life skill that we all need to define, practice, use, and internalize. We use self-control because it makes us feel good about ourselves. Rather than giving children external rewards for using their self-control, make it known that they are using their self-control to make themselves feel good. Help students who are having problems using their self-control by noticing and praising the times they do use self-control and by helping them get their self-control back through Self-Control Time, a specific technique described in Lesson 4.*

Although it is ultimately up to each student to use his or her self-control, we must provide positive reminders that it takes self-control to participate in many daily activities. Some examples of situations requiring self-control include the following:

▶ Raising your hand to wait your turn to speak

▶ Staying focused on your work

▶ Keeping your hands to yourself

▶ Walking quietly in the hallway

▶ Playing by the rules in gym class

▶ Cleaning your room

▶ Telling the truth

▶ Trying your best

Daily Guidelines for Self-Control

▶ Provide positive reminders that students must use their self-control.

▶ Convey the message that using their self-control makes people feel proud of themselves.

---

*Self-Control Time is a registered trademark of Lesson One Company.

▶ Help students who are having problems using their self-control by noticing and praising them when they do.

▶ Use Self-Control Time to help individual students who need to get their self-control back.

▶ Use Self-Control Time to help the entire class refocus and regain their self-control.

LESSON 1

Introducing Self-Control

OBJECTIVE   Students will define and experience the skill of Self-Control.

MATERIALS
- ▶ Self-Control poster (Appendix C)
- ▶ A drum (or another musical instrument)
- ▶ *For the first-grade extension:* Crayons or markers, drawing paper

PROCEDURE   *Before teaching this lesson, hang the Self-Control poster in a prominent location in your classroom. Leave the poster up for future reference.*

STEP 1 —— **Introduce the skill of Self-Control.**

Referring to the poster, read the parts of the Self-Control skill to your class.

Self-Control

Self-control is when I am in charge of what I do and what I say.

I use my self-control to listen and follow directions.

Using self-control helps me not do things that may be harmful to myself and others.

Self-control helps me stay safe, be successful, and create peace.

STEP 2 —— **Give an example of how you, as an adult, use the skill of Self-Control.**

For example, you might say that instead of yelling at your kids when you are irritated, you try to talk calmly to them.

STEP 3 —— **Give examples of ways students can use the skill of Self-Control at home, at school, and in the community.**

Explain that it takes self-control to listen and follow directions and to follow the Pledge for Peace. For example:

Home: Treating your brother or sister the way you'd like to be treated

School: Waiting to give an answer when the teacher asks you a question

Community: Recycling your cans instead of putting them in the trash

Ask students to describe additional situations in which they have (or have not) used their self-control.

STEP 4 —— **Discuss the idea that students are responsible for their own self-control.**

Share the following thoughts:

> Suppose a teacher has given a direction for all students to use their listening and try their best not to talk. A person next to you taps you on the shoulder and starts talking to you. If you talk back, who made you lose your self-control?

Discuss the fact that it is up to the students to use their self-control, even if someone else is bothering them.

Ask questions such as the following:

▶ Who makes you talk? Who makes you raise your hand?

▶ Whose responsibility is it to use self-control?

STEP 5 —— **Have students experience the skill of Self-Control by playing a game.**

Who Made You Move?

Purpose of the game

In this game, students will use their self-control to move their bodies only when they hear the drum (or other musical instrument). When the drum stops, students must use their self-control to stop moving. Students will understand that it is up to them to control their bodies.

How to play

First, allow the students to hear and see the drum. Choose a body part that the students will shake (hands, shoulders, elbows, knees, and so on). Tell the group that when they hear the sound, they should shake the body part chosen. When the sound stops, the students must use their self-control to stop moving and remain still until they hear the sound again.

The speed of the game can be varied. The body part that students are shaking can be varied as well. When telling students to use a different part of the body, remind them they are using self-control to listen to your directions.

After the game is over, you can discuss the following ideas:

▶ Who made you move? Was it me, the instrument, or you? *(you)* That is called self-control. It is up to you to use your self-control.

▶ Who makes you call out or raise your hand when you have something to say? *(you do)* It takes self-control to raise your hand and wait to speak.

▶ If someone is bothering you, and you call the person a mean name, who makes you call that person the name? *(you do)* It is up to you to use your self-control to treat others the way you would like to be treated.

STEP 6 —— **Do the Using Self-Control activity.**

Have students turn to page 24 in their Student Manuals (Using Self-Control). Instruct them to draw a line between the people who are not using their self-control and the people who are. Briefly discuss why the students responded the way they did.

First-grade extension: Ask students to come up with other situations and draw another set of examples on a separate page.

Reinforcing Self-Control

OBJECTIVE   Students will further explore the skill of Self-Control and apply it to their lives.

MATERIALS
- ▶ Red and green construction paper (a small square of each color for every student)
- ▶ Copies of the I Control Myself activity (page 80)
- ▶ Crayons or markers

PROCEDURE

STEP 1 —— **Review what the class learned about the skill of Self-Control in the previous lesson.**

Referring to the Self-Control poster, review the skill. Discuss the idea that everyone, whether adult or child, must use this skill to be successful at home, at school, and in the community.

Ask students what they learned from the game in the previous lesson (Who Made You Move?).

STEP 2 —— **Encourage students to experience the skill of Self-Control by playing the following game.**

Walk Away with Self-Control

Purpose of the game

When given the example of a situation in which one student is calling another student names, the class will describe responses that the student being teased might make. They will distinguish between responses that do show self-control and responses that don't by holding up a red or green construction-paper card.

How to play

Explain that you will be playing a game to show how students can use their self-control and what happens when they don't. Give each student a red square and a green square of construction paper.

Read the following situation aloud:

> Tim and Rashida are playing on the swing set during recess. When no adults are around, Tim begins to make fun of Rashida by calling her names. Rashida does not know what to do. What could she do?

Ask students to think of answers to the question. Explain that if a student volunteers an answer that uses self-control, the student's classmates hold up the green card. If a student gives an answer that does not show self-control, the student's classmates hold up the red card. If a response does not show self-control, discuss what the result of that response is likely to be.

After the game is over, you can ask the following questions:

▶ Are kids like Tim—who call people names, push, and fight—using their self-control?

▶ How many people does it take to fight? *(more than one)*

▶ What did Rashida do that showed she was using her self-control? *(walking away, telling an adult, and so forth)*

▶ How can using your self-control help you create peace in your life?

▶ Who should you be proud of when you use your self-control?

STEP 3 —— **Do the I Control Myself activity.**

Have students turn to page 25 in their Student Manuals and discuss the ways in which the children in the three situations pictured are using their self-control. Let students know that the fourth example has a question mark because they will need to draw a picture of their own self-control situation.

Give each student a copy of the I Control Myself activity, and distribute the crayons or markers. Encourage students to draw a picture of a time when they used their self-control.

After students have finished, ask for volunteers to share their drawings with the class. If you wish, post the drawings on a bulletin board or the classroom wall.

I Control Myself

LESSON 3

Learning through Literature:
Self-Control Stories

OBJECTIVE   Students will relate what they have learned about the skill of Self-Control to a story from the life of Louis D. Brown.

MATERIALS
▶ Crayons or markers

▶ Copies of the Self-Control Home Page (Appendix D)

▶ *Optional:* A copy of the story you choose to read to the class for each student to keep or take home.

▶ *Optional:* Photographs of students' role models, glue

PROCEDURE

STEP 1 —— **Read the Louis D. Brown story about self-control that is best suited to your class.**

Louis and the Lollipop

—Recommended for kindergarten. Before reading, explain that this is a story in the form of a poem.

Synopsis: Louis is sick and goes to the principal's office to wait for his mother. While he's sitting there, he finds himself drawn to a jar of lollipops on the principal's desk. Even though he loves lollipops, he uses his self-control and resists the temptation to take one. When his mother comes to get him, he can't help but be proud of himself for using his self-control.

Read the poem on page 84.

After reading the poem, discuss how it relates to the skill of Self-Control. You can ask the following questions:

▶ Why did Louis decide not to take a lollipop from the jar?

► How can you stop yourself from taking something that is not yours?

► Have you ever stopped yourself from doing something by using your self-control? Tell about it.

The Cookie Bandit

—Recommended for first grade

Synopsis: Louis's mother is throwing him a birthday party and leaves a plate of cookies unattended. They're his favorite kind, so despite her warning, Louis ends up eating the whole plate. Later that day, he gets sick and sees that his mom was right and that he needed to use his self-control.

Read the story on pages 85–86.

After the story is over, discuss how it relates to self-control. You can ask the following questions:

► Louis's mom told him not to eat the cookies until the party began, but he didn't listen and ate them behind her back. If you were in Louis's shoes, what would you have done?

► By the time the guests arrived, Louis had already lost his self-control and eaten most of the cookies. Do you think this was fair to the other children who might have wanted some, too?

► At the end of the story, Louis gets sick and can't play the games at his birthday party. Do you think he learned his lesson?

► In the story, Louis showed no self-control. Why do you think self-control is so important?

STEP 2 —— **Do the Self-Control Role Model activity.**

Have students turn to page 26 in their Student Manuals (Self-Control Role Model). Encourage students to choose someone at home, at school, or in the community who is a role model for self-control. Remind students that a role model is someone who sets a good example for others.

Have students draw a picture of the person they chose in the frame.

If photographs of these people are available, students may glue these to the page.

After students have finished, ask for volunteers to share their choices with the class.

First-grade extension: Have students write down, on the lines provided, the reason they chose this person as their self-control role model.

STEP 3 —— **Assign the Self-Control Home Page.**

Give students a copy of the Self-Control Home Page to share with parents or caregivers.

Louis and the Lollipop

Joseph M. Chéry

Louis D. Brown feels a bit sick.
His throat is real scratchy—he hopes his mom comes quick!
The nurse takes him to the principal's office and closes the door
    with a "click."

He sits in the big chair in the principal's office, just looking around,
when he spots a jar of lollipops, just waiting to be found!
He lifts the glass lid, not making a sound.

Inside he can see lollipops of all colors—red, blue, and green!
All of his favorite flavors, oh, how lucky is he!
He licks his lips, imagining how tasty a blue lolly will be.

Suddenly, he stops, frozen in place by a vision of Ms. Knoll,
his first-grade teacher, who said just this morning,
"Louis, remember your self-control!"

Louis thinks of how bad he would feel, knowing that he stole.
Because he knows the lollipops are not his to eat,
he puts the lid down and heads back to his seat.

"I must use my self-control," he constantly repeats.
He takes a deep breath, closes his eyes, relaxing himself,
thinking how proud he'll be for resisting the lolly right there on the shelf.

Not only that, he thinks with a smile, the lolly isn't good for my health!
Louis D. Brown is sitting like that, with his eyes closed, feet on the floor,
when he hears a knock at the door.

His mom appears and says, "Oh, my poor dear, is your throat sore?"
"It is, Mom, but guess what?"
"Louis, did you take a lollipop?" Mom says with a tut.

"No, I used my self-control and didn't!" says Louis as he leaves the office with
    a strut.

The Cookie Bandit

Blue Telusma

I love cookies. Especially chocolate chip cookies. That's why when I woke up from my nap and smelled them baking in the oven, I jumped off the couch and ran into the kitchen.

"What are those for?" I asked, watching Mom pull them out of the oven. Mom doesn't like me eating too many sweets, so she only makes them on special occasions.

"They're for your birthday party later. I made an extra batch because I know how carried away you get sometimes."

"Can I have some now?"

"No, not yet, Louis. You need to have some self-control and wait till everyone gets here," Mom said.

"Aw, man," I thought. "Just my luck!"

All day, I kept walking by the kitchen, hoping to grab a couple of cookies while Mom wasn't watching. But there always seemed to be someone in there. I was going crazy waiting for the guests to arrive so I could dig into my treats. So when the doorbell finally rang, I ran straight for the snack table while my mom was letting people in.

First I grabbed two cookies while she put away the kids' coats. Then I grabbed some more while she was talking on the phone to Nana. By the time the party started, I had eaten most of the plate of cookies by myself, and they were good.

That's when Uncle Jeff came into the living room and said that it was time to play musical chairs. I love musical chairs, so I ran to the middle of the room with the rest of the kids.

Over and over, we danced around in a circle and then rushed to sit down when the music stopped. Everyone was laughing and having fun. And I was happy because I was winning. There were only four people left in the game, and I was sure I'd beat them all.

The Cookie Bandit *(continued)*

But then all of a sudden I started to get a funny feeling in my tummy. Every time I moved, I felt sick, and when the music stopped this time, instead of sitting down, I threw up all over the carpet.

I was so embarrassed! Mom took me to the bathroom while Uncle Jeff cleaned up the mess.

For the rest of the party, I had to sit down while everyone else kept playing and having fun. Later on, when Mom found out that I'd eaten all those cookies, she said that's why I had gotten sick.

I still love sweets, but I'll try to use my self-control next time because you can have too much of a good thing.

Introducing Self-Control Time

OBJECTIVE   Students will learn and practice Self-Control Time.

MATERIALS   ▶ Self-Control Time poster (Appendix C)

PROCEDURE   *Before teaching this lesson, hang the Self-Control Time poster in a prominent location in your classroom. Leave the poster up for future reference.*

STEP 1 — **Introduce Self-Control Time.**

Referring to the poster, present the description of Self-Control Time.

Self-Control Time

Self-Control Time is a fun breathing exercise to help me calm down, focus, and get my self-control back.

You can discuss the following ideas:

▶ Self-Control Time is a positive and natural way that we can calm ourselves down.

▶ We all lose our self-control at some time, and Self-Control Time is a way that we can get it back.

STEP 2 — **Help students experience Self-Control Time by leading them through the process.**

Whole-Class Self-Control Time

1. Sit comfortably with your back against the chair.

2. Place your feet flat on the floor in front of you.

3. Place your hands so they are resting gently on your lap.

4. Relax your shoulders so the muscles around them are not tight or tense.

5. Breathe deeply through your nose and exhale through your mouth.

6. Close your eyelids lightly and focus on your breathing.

Let students know that the steps in Self-Control Time appear on page 27 in their Student Manuals.

Students who are having difficulty doing Self-Control Time or who have emotional problems will need more help and support. These students might need to learn Self-Control Time in smaller steps or smaller groups.

STEP 3 —— **Identify situations in which the whole class could use Self-Control Time.**

Ask students what different things they do when they get up in the morning. *(eat breakfast, get dressed, brush teeth, feed a pet, pack up school materials, and so forth)* Point out that because they are doing so many things to get ready, it is natural to want to calm themselves down first thing when they get to the classroom.

Let students know that it is also natural to want to calm down at times they might be excited about something. *(for instance, a school assembly or class party)*

Ask students for other times they think using Self-Control Time as a class would be helpful. *(for example, after lunch or recess)*

Self-Control Time for the whole class, as a regular part of the day, takes approximately three minutes.

STEP 4 —— **Introduce individual Self-Control Time.**

Let students know that if a person loses his or her self-control, that person can take Self-Control Time right in his or her seat. Explain that this is not a punishment, just a way for a student to get back his or her self-control.

When a teacher tells an individual student to use Self-Control Time to help regain self-control, the student breathes quietly for thirty to sixty seconds.

STEP 5 —— **Introduce and demonstrate Individual Self-Control Time with a student volunteer.**

Ask for a volunteer to help you with the following demonstration.

Individual Self-Control Time

1. If a student is not using self-control, begin by reminding the student to use his or her self-control.

2. If the student has not regained self-control, use your limit-setting voice and say, "Please take a Self-Control Time to get your self-control back."

   Remember, the student can do Self-Control Time wherever he or she is—not in a special chair or area.

3. Remind the student that Self-Control Time is not a punishment but an opportunity to regain self-control.

4. Have the student sit up straight, breathe deeply through the nose, and exhale through the mouth.

5. In a firm but kind voice, calmly ask the student to open his or her eyes. Ask, "Who controls you?" Make sure the student realizes that it is up to him or her to use self-control.

6. Encourage the student to feel proud for getting his or her self-control back.

STEP 6 —— **Have the students experience the skill of Self-Control by playing the following game.**

Listen for Self-Control

Purpose of the game

Students will practice using their self-control to listen and follow directions.

How to play

First, tell students that they will be practicing using their self-control to listen and follow directions. Second, using the word *self-control* in a sentence, give the students a direction to follow. For example:

▶ Use your *self-control* by putting your hands on your heads.

▶ Use your *self-control* by standing up.

▶ Use your *self-control* by clapping your hands.

▶ Use your *self-control* to stop clapping your hands.

As in the game Simon Says, if you do not use the word *self-control* in the direction you give, the students should not follow that direction. Remind students that it is okay to make mistakes as long as they keep trying their best and learn from their mistakes. (If more than one adult is in the room, you can take turns giving directions.)

Mentioning this game when you are giving students directions throughout the day helps remind them that they must use their self-control to follow your instructions.

Do a whole-class Self-Control Time.

Tell students that because the fun game they have been playing is over, it's time for them to calm down, refocus, and practice Self-Control Time. Follow the directions given earlier for the whole-class Self-Control Time.

LESSON 5

Community Service Learning: Seeds of Peace

OBJECTIVE   Students will apply the skill of Self-Control as they complete a community service project.

MATERIALS

▶ A copy of the book *The Empty Pot,* by Demi (New York: Henry Holt, 1990)

▶ Marigold seeds, potting soil, peat pots or paper cups, watering cans

▶ Garden trowels and a place in the schoolyard for the plants

PROCEDURE   *If you are unable to locate a copy of the book, you can read or para-phrase the synopsis instead.*

STEP 1 —— **Remind students of the meaning of *community* and *community service.***

Ask students to tell you the meaning of the words *community* (a group of people who work together) and *community service* (things we do to give to our community).

STEP 2 —— **Introduce the project.**

Let students know that they will be doing a community service project that involves beautifying the school by planting and growing flowers. To set the stage, read Ping's story aloud.

Synopsis: An emperor in China needs to choose a successor to his throne. So he gives all the children in the kingdom a seed and tells them that they are to return in a year with their plants. The emperor says that in one year, he will look at the plants and pick a new emperor according to how the plants look. One year later, all of the children return with beautiful plants, except for one child named Ping. Ping tries his best to make the plant grow, but the plant does not grow. He returns to the emperor with an empty pot. When the emperor sees the empty pot, he chooses Ping to be his successor because all of the seeds had been boiled, and none of them should have grown. Ping was the only one honest enough to return with an empty pot.

When you have finished reading, you can ask questions such as the following:

- ▶ How does Ping use his self-control?
- ▶ Why is it important to be honest?
- ▶ How does being honest make our classroom community a more peaceful place to be?
- ▶ Do you want your friends to be honest with you?
- ▶ Why is it hard to be honest sometimes?

S T E P 3 —— **Do the project.**

Distribute the marigold seeds and potting materials and show the students how to pot up the seeds. Have each student plant a pot with three or four seeds.

Discuss how the flowers are a community service because, when they bloom, they will add beauty to the schoolyard. Point out to the students that, as in the story, not every flower will bloom: What is important is that they try their best to nurture the plants and have the self-control to wait for them to grow.

Place the pots in a sunny location; then have students water them every week and watch their progress.

S T E P 4 —— **Present the project.**

When the plants are big enough, hold a ceremony to transplant them in the schoolyard. Invite other members of the school community to the ceremony if you wish.

S T E P 5 —— **Take time to reflect on the project.**

You can ask the following questions.

General questions
- ▶ What was doing this project like for you?

► Which part of the project did you like the least? The most?

► What parts of the Pledge for Peace did you use while you were doing this project?

► What other Peacezone skills did you use?

Responses to the last two questions can include any and all of the aspects of the Pledge for Peace and the skills of Trying Your Best and Self-Control.

► How did you feel when you finished the project?

Specific questions

► When did you use your self-control during this project? *(for example, when planting the seeds and waiting for them to grow, when waiting for a turn to transplant the potted plants in the schoolyard)*

► How did you feel when you used your self-control? *(proud)*

► What do you think the rest of the school might have learned about the skill of Self-Control?

► Can you think of any other ways we could help the people in our school use their self-control?

UNIT 5

Thinking and Problem Solving

Throughout the day, students solve a range of problems that vary from answering questions in class to getting along at recess. When students practice thinking of a variety of ways to solve a problem, they learn to think "outside the box." Rather than giving up when they have a problem to solve, students can use their thinking skills to generate all the possible solutions to a problem. When a problem arises at school, at home, or in the community, they can choose from among these possibilities to solve the problem in a peaceful manner.

Thinking and problem solving are skills that children and adults use constantly. Although it is up to each student to use his or her thinking skills to solve problems, we can remind students to try their best and think of all the different ways a problem could be solved.

Some examples of situations in which students use thinking and problem-solving skills include the following:

► Answering a question in class

► Doing a science experiment

► Resolving a disagreement with a classmate

► Discussing a story

► Deciding what movie to watch

Daily Guidelines for Thinking and Problem Solving

► Remind students to think of all the different ways they could possibly solve a problem.

► Provide positive reminders when a student is trying to solve a problem.

► Reinforce the idea that instead of giving up on a problem, students should keep thinking until they solve the problem.

► Praise students for trying their best immediately after they use their thinking and problem-solving skills.

Introducing Thinking and Problem Solving

OBJECTIVE   Students will define and experience the skills of Thinking and Problem Solving.

MATERIALS
- ▶ Thinking and Problem-Solving poster (Appendix C)
- ▶ *For the game:* A brown paper bag and a selection of small objects that can be placed in the bag
- ▶ *For the first-grade extension:* Chalkboard or easel pad

PROCEDURE   *Before teaching this lesson, post the Thinking and Problem-Solving poster in a prominent location in your classroom. Leave the poster up for future reference.*

STEP 1 —— **Introduce the skills of Thinking and Problem Solving to the class.**

Referring to the poster, read the parts of the Thinking and Problem-Solving skills aloud to the class.

Thinking and Problem Solving

Thinking is when I come up with as many ideas as I can.

Problem solving is when I think in order to find the solution to a problem.

I keep thinking until I solve the problem. I don't give up.

Thinking and problem solving help me find ways to create peace.

Explain to your class that when they have a problem and don't know the answer, they can use the skills of Thinking and Problem

Solving. Instead of giving up or saying, "I can't do this," they can think of all the different ways it is possible to solve a problem.

STEP 2 — **Give examples of how you, as an adult, use the skills of Thinking and Problem Solving in your life.**

For example, you might say you use these skills when you decide how to teach the students a new math lesson.

STEP 3 — **Give examples of ways students can use the skills of Thinking and Problem Solving at home, at school, and in the community.**

Explain that both adults and children must use these skills throughout the day and in many different places.

Home: Solving a sharing problem with your brother or sister

School: Planning a Peace Day celebration

Community: Helping your neighbors keep your street clean

Ask students to give additional examples, if they can; then discuss the following ideas:

▶ We are all smart. When we try to solve a problem, our ideas can be like fireworks going off in our brains, one right after the other.

▶ We keep thinking until we can find a solution. Once we think we have one, we can give it a try. It's okay if we make a mistake. If one idea doesn't work, we can try another one.

STEP 4 — **Discuss how Self-Control Time can help students use the skills of Thinking and Problem Solving.**

Discuss with students times when it is hard for them to think (for example, when they are worried, don't feel safe, or are thinking about a lot of things at once).

Let students know that they can use Self-Control Time to help them calm down and focus so they can think better.

Referring to the Self-Control Time poster, review the individual use of Self-Control Time. Demonstrate this technique with a student volunteer, if necessary.

Directions for Self-Control Time appear on page 89 in this book and on page 27 in the Student Manual.

STEP 5 — **Have students experience the skills of Thinking and Problem Solving by playing the following game.**

What's in the Bag?

Purpose of the game

Students will use thinking and problem solving to guess what an object is when they cannot see it. Generating multiple possibilities will help students learn that they can think creatively when they are attempting to solve problems at home, at school, or in the community.

How to play

Place a fairly common object (i.e., an orange, a fruit juice box, a piggy bank) in a plain brown paper bag. Tell students they must guess what is in the bag by feeling or shaking the bag. Hold the bag so each student can feel, but not see, what is inside. Remind students to use their self-control when they touch the bag and to wait their turn to say what they think the object is.

After each student has had a chance to feel the object, go around the room and ask students what they think the object is and why: Did they identify it by its shape? Its texture? Was it hot or cold? Did it make noise?

After the game is over, you can ask the following questions:

► In the game, you had to think of a lot of different things the object might be. When do you sometimes have to think of a lot of different ways to solve a problem?

► If you have a problem to solve, should you give up, or should you think of all the different ways you can solve it?

STEP 6 — **Do the Thinking in New Ways activity.**

Have students turn to page 30 in their Student Manuals (Thinking in New Ways). Encourage them to use the line on this page to create any drawing that they would like (an animal, a roller coaster, waves on an ocean, and so forth).

When the students have finished drawing, ask for volunteers to share their pictures with the class. Emphasize that students created a number of different things, just as there are many different ways to solve a problem.

First-grade extension: Put a similar line on an easel pad or chalk-board and have students come up one at a time and contribute to a group picture.

LESSON 2

Reinforcing Thinking and Problem Solving

OBJECTIVE   Students will further explore thinking and problem solving and will apply the Five Steps of Thinking and Problem Solving.

MATERIALS
- ► Five Steps of Thinking and Problem-Solving poster (Appendix C)
- ► *For the game:* A ruler or similar object (yardstick, rhythm stick, pointer)

PROCEDURE   *Before teaching this lesson, post the Five Steps of Thinking and Problem-Solving poster in a prominent location in your classroom. Leave the poster up for future reference.*

STEP 1 —— **Review what students learned in the previous lesson about the skills of Thinking and Problem Solving.**

Review the skills of Thinking and Problem Solving, as described on the poster. Discuss the idea that both children and adults use these skills many times in their daily lives.

Ask students to tell you what they learned from the game they played in the previous lesson (What's in the Bag?).

STEP 2 —— **Play the following game to reinforce the skills of Thinking and Problem Solving.**

What Else Can This Be?

Purpose of the game

Students will use their thinking and problem-solving skills to come up with a number of ideas about what a simple object might be. Generating many possibilities will help students learn to think creatively when they are attempting to solve a problem.

How to play

Tell students that you are going to play a fun game to challenge their thinking and problem-solving abilities. Hold up the ruler or other item in front of the class. Explain that they know what this item is *(a ruler)* but that you want to know all the other things that it could be. Give students a few examples. *(a baseball bat, a hairbrush, a moustache)*

Next ask students what else they think the object could be. Let them know that there are no right or wrong answers: The challenge is to think creatively and come up with as many ideas as they can.

Have them raise their hands when they have an idea. Encourage them to keep thinking of as many things as they can and remind them that their ideas can be like fireworks going off.

After you have completed this activity, you can vary the game by asking students what a specific sound could be. For example, you could crumple a piece of paper and challenge students to think of all the different things that could make that sound. You could also vary the game by holding up other objects—for example, a ball, a sheet of paper, or a bean bag.

After the game is over, ask questions like the following:

▶ Was it easy or hard to think of things the object(s) could be? Why?

▶ How did you use your thinking and problem solving to decide what the object could be?

STEP 3 —— **Ask students to identify times they need to remind themselves to think of all the different ways they can solve a problem.**

Ask questions like the following:

▶ When have you used your thinking to solve a challenging problem?

▶ If you have a problem with a friend, how could you use your thinking to solve it?

STEP 4 —— **Introduce the Five Steps of Thinking and Problem Solving.**

Five Steps of Thinking and Problem Solving

Step 1: What is the problem?

Step 2: What are my choices?

Step 3: What are the consequences of my choices? (What could happen?)

Step 4: Make a choice.

Step 5: How did I do?

STEP 5 —— **Apply the Five Steps of Thinking and Problem Solving to a common situation.**

Referring to the Five Steps of Thinking and Problem-Solving poster, ask students to imagine that they are on the playground and someone is calling them mean names.

Go through each of the five steps to illustrate the process of thinking and problem solving.

Step 1: What is the problem?   Someone is calling you names.

Step 2: What are my choices?
- a. Call the person a name.
- b. Hit the person.
- c. Walk away.
- d. Get a teacher.
- e. Tell the person to leave you alone.

Step 3: What are the consequences of my choices? (What could happen?)
- a. The person will call me another name.
- b. The person will hit me.
- c. The person will follow me.
- d. The person will call me a tattle-tale.
- e. The person will leave me alone.

Step 4: Make a choice.

Step 5: How did I do?

Let students know that they have a copy of the steps in their Student Manuals on page 31.

Have students turn to page 32 in their Student Manuals (Sara's Playground Problem). Discuss each step with the class and have them predict the outcomes of each choice.

Have students draw a line from Sara to the choice they think Sara should make, then ask the students how Sara did: Did her choice solve the problem?

First-grade extension: Have a volunteer come up with another scenario and talk through the five-step process as a class.

Learning through Literature: Thinking and Problem-Solving Stories

OBJECTIVE Students will relate what they have learned about thinking and problem solving to a story from the life of Louis D. Brown.

MATERIALS
- ▶ Copies of the Thinking and Problem-Solving Home Page (Appendix D)
- ▶ *Optional:* A copy of the story you choose to read to the class for each student to keep or take home
- ▶ *Optional:* Photographs of students' role models, glue

PROCEDURE

STEP 1 —— **Read the Louis D. Brown story about thinking and problem solving that is best suited to your class.**

The Sand Castle

—*Recommended for kindergarten*

Synopsis: At the beach, Louis starts building a sand castle but is disappointed that he doesn't have any tools to help him make it. While getting some juice from his mom, he realizes that he can use a plastic cup instead of a bucket. Fueled by his new idea, he goes back to his spot in the sand and builds a beautiful castle.

The New Airplane

—*Recommended for first grade*

Synopsis: Louis wants to play with the classroom's new toy airplane during free play. Unfortunately, his classmate Jasmine gets to the plane before he does, and Louis becomes very upset. When his teacher finds out what has happened, she suggests that Louis think of a solution to his problem rather than just let his anger get the best of him.

Read The Sand Castle (pages 107–108) or The New Airplane (pages 109–110).

After you have finished reading, refer to the Five Steps of Thinking and Problem-Solving poster and discuss the story:

Step 1: What was Louis's problem?

Step 2: What were his choices? (What different choices did he have?)

Step 3: What were the consequences of those choices? (What could happen after each choice?)

Step 4: What was Louis's choice? (Would you have chosen that one? Why or why not?)

Step 5: How did Louis do? (Did his choice solve the problem?)

You can also relate the story to the students' own experiences:

► Have you ever had a problem like Louis's?

► What did you do to solve it?

► Did anyone help you solve the problem?

STEP 2 —— **Do the Thinking and Problem-Solving Role Model activity.**

Have students turn to page 33 in their Student Manuals (Thinking and Problem-Solving Role Model) and invite them to choose someone from home, school, or community who is a role model for thinking and problem solving. Remind students that a role model is someone who sets a good example for other people.

Have students draw a picture of that person.

If photographs of these people are available, students may glue these to the page.

After students have finished drawing, ask for volunteers to share their pictures with the class.

First-grade extension: Help students write down the reason(s) they chose this person as their role model for thinking and problem solving.

STEP 3 —— **Assign the Thinking and Problem-Solving Home Page.**

Give students a copy of the Thinking and Problem-Solving Home Page to share with their parents or caregivers.

The Sand Castle

Blue Telusma

It was a lovely summer day, and Louis was at the beach with his family. He was sitting on the hot sand, looking at the blue ocean. His feet played with the water and the sand, mixing them together every time a wave came.

Louis decided to have some fun. He was going to build a sand castle. He had built one before, so he knew what to do. He would dig up some sand, pile it up, and then shape it into walls and towers.

Louis looked into his backpack for something to use to build his sand castle. The last time he built a sand castle, he used a small shovel and a bucket. He had forgotten to bring them to the beach.

"How could he build his sand castle?" Louis wondered. He needed a shovel to scoop up the sand. He needed a bucket to carry the sand and shape the sand into round towers. But tools or no tools, Louis was determined to build a sand castle.

He selected a good spot away from the water and began to work. He scooped up some sand with his fingers and carried the sand to the spot. But Louis had small hands, so he could only carry a very small amount of sand at one time.

Louis wanted to build a large sand castle. He would have to scoop up and carry a lot of sand in his small hands. It was hot on the beach, and Louis was getting tired. Soon his fingers began to hurt, and he still did not have enough sand for his castle.

Hot and disappointed, Louis decided to go back to where his parents were resting to get a cold drink out of their picnic basket.

"How's the sand castle coming along?" his father asked when he saw Louis approaching.

"Not very well," Louis replied, pouting. "I'm exhausted. Can I have something to drink?"

Feeling bad for her son, Louis's mother took out a pitcher of juice and poured him a big cup. Louis was so hot and thirsty he gulped the juice down in a matter of seconds. Then he asked his mom for a second cup. As he was sitting there with his father, watching her pour the juice, suddenly he got an idea.

The Sand Castle *(continued)*

"Hey, Mom, can I have that cup when I'm done?" he asked, getting excited.

"Sure," she replied. "But why would you want to keep an empty plastic cup?"

"To use in place of a bucket!" Louis proudly replied.

All morning he had tried his other options. He'd scooped up as much sand as he could in his hands, and that hadn't worked very well. He'd thought of giving up on building the sand castle altogether, but Louis wasn't a quitter, so that idea wasn't so great either. Using his plastic cup as a bucket seemed like the best choice.

After he finished drinking his last bit of juice, Louis ran back to his sand castle and began to work with a new burst of energy. For the next hour, he would scoop up sand in his cup and carry it to the spot where he was building his castle. Slowly but surely, he had a high pile of sand without being as tired as he had been the first time around. He then patted down the sand into the cup and flipped it upside down to let the sand out. With each cup of gathered sand, he began to form a nice round tower.

Quietly, Louis worked until he had built a castle with ten towers, placed side by side in a circle. For the finishing touch, he used his fingers to dig out little holes around the top of each tower to make windows. The sand castle was complete.

Louis stood back for a second and admired his work. He couldn't believe how beautiful it was. Even though he hadn't come to the beach with the right tools to build his castle, through the process of thinking he came up with the best solution to his problem and got the job done successfully.

Louis was proud of himself for thinking and problem solving, and he ran to tell his parents to come see his sand castle. When they saw what he had built, they were proud of him, too. He had not given up, and now he had something to show for it.

The New Airplane

Joseph M. Chéry

It was time for free play in Ms. Walker's first-grade class. Louis looked forward to free play every day. There were so many things he enjoyed doing, he never knew which center he should go to first! Should he go to the coloring area and use the crayons and construction paper to make a huge, noisy airplane? Or should he go to the book corner and read the book with all of the pictures of airplanes? Louis loved airplanes—he wanted to fly around the world when he grew up.

Louis was standing in the middle of the classroom, daydreaming about flying planes, when he spotted a brand-new toy in the block area. It was shiny and gray and made a whirring noise that Louis could hear across the room. The new toy was an airplane! Louis was so excited that he wanted to run right over to the airplane, but he remembered he had to use his self-control and walk in the classroom. Louis used his self-control and walked as quickly as he could across the room. He never took his eyes off the airplane.

At the very moment when Louis reached out his hand to pick up the plane, Jasmine Jackson grabbed the plane with both hands! She took the plane and walked over to her friend Sam, waving the airplane in the air. Louis was very angry. He saw the airplane first and was about to play with it when Jasmine ran over. He went up to Jasmine and said, "I was coming to use that airplane!"

"Too bad. I got there first," Jasmine said, holding the plane above her head.

Louis didn't know what to do. He thought about hitting Jasmine or yelling at her to get her to drop the plane. But he remembered about using his self-control and that if he lost his self-control he would only make Jasmine feel bad, and he would not feel very good about himself. What could he do?

He was sitting on the floor with his head in his hands when Ms. Walker came over and asked him what was wrong. Louis explained what had happened with Jasmine and the airplane. Ms. Walker told Louis he did a great job with his self-control and that now he and Jasmine just needed to use their thinking to solve the problem. Ms. Walker reminded Louis that free play had just started and that there would be plenty of time for both Jasmine and Louis to play with the airplane. Ms. Walker asked Louis if he could think of some ways that both he and Jasmine could use the plane.

The New Airplane *(continued)*

Louis thought for a few minutes, and then he dried his eyes on his sleeve, stood up, and went over to where Jasmine and Sam were playing with the airplane.

"Jasmine, can I play with the airplane when you're done?" asked Louis politely. "I have lots of great ideas about how we could share the airplane and play together, too."

"Sure," said Jasmine. "I will be done in one minute, and then maybe you can be the pilot on the airplane and Sam and I can be the passengers!"

Louis felt much better. He had used his thinking to solve his problem and helped to keep peace with his friends. He was so proud of himself, he couldn't wait to go home and tell his mother, brother, and sister how he solved his problem during free time!

Community Service Learning: Thinking through Service

OBJECTIVE Students will apply the skills of Thinking and Problem Solving as they complete a community service project.

MATERIALS
- ▶ A copy of the book *The Squiggle,* by Carole Lexa Schaefer (Edmund, OK: Dragonfly Publishing, 1999)
- ▶ Different-colored construction paper, glue, crayons or markers

PROCEDURE *Before doing this lesson, assemble enough sheets of construction paper for each student to have one. Cut out the same number of construction-paper circles (an inch or two in diameter). If you are unable to locate the book referred to in this lesson, you can read and discuss the synopsis instead.*

STEP 1 —— **Remind students of the meaning of *community* and *community service*.**

Ask students to tell you the meaning of the words *community* (a group of people who work together) and *community service* (things we do to give to our community).

STEP 2 —— **Introduce the project.**

Let students know that they will be doing a community service project that involves making special drawings to hang in a public area of the school or in a place in the community.

To set the stage, read the story *The Squiggle*.

Synopsis: When a group of children set off with their teacher on an orderly walk through the park, the very last little girl spies a "squiggle" (a long red ribbon) on the ground and picks it up. As she twirls, twists, and turns this ribbon, she imagines it to be a dragon, a thundercloud, a "full fat moon," and much more. She joins the group again and shows them all the things her ribbon can be. The children continue their walk, not as a "bunched-up, slow, tight, straight line." Instead, they walk "squiggle-style."

After you have finished reading, ask questions like the following:

▶ What do you think it means to walk "squiggle-style"? *(happily, wiggling, in many different ways)*

▶ How did the girl in the story use her thinking and imagination?

▶ What things did the girl turn the ribbon into?

▶ What other things do you think the ribbon could become?

STEP 3 —— **Do the project.**

Give each student a sheet and circle of construction paper (of different colors) and distribute the glue and crayons or markers. Explain how to do the project:

> You will be using your thinking skills to decide what to draw on your sheet of construction paper. You may draw anything you like. However, you must glue the paper circle somewhere in your drawing and use your imagination to turn the circle into something that is part of the picture.

Students' drawings might be, for example, of a flower, a lion, or a house. The circles in these drawings might then become the sun shining on the flower, the lion's face, and a soccer ball a child is kicking in front of a house.

After students have finished, encourage them to share their drawings and talk about how they thought about and chose a way to use the circles.

STEP 4 —— **Present the project.**

Arrange to have students hang their pictures in a public place in the school or in a nursing home, hospital, or other community location.

STEP 5 —— **Take time to reflect on the project.**

You can ask the following questions.

General questions

▶ What was doing this project like for you?

▶ Which part of the project did you like the least? The most?

▶ What parts of the Pledge for Peace did you use while you were doing this project?

▶ What other Peacezone skills did you use?

Responses to the last two questions can include any and all of the aspects of the Pledge for Peace and the skills of Trying Your Best, Self-Control, and Thinking and Problem Solving.

▶ How did you feel when you finished the project?

Specific questions

▶ When did you use your thinking and problem-solving skills during this project?

▶ How did you feel when you used your thinking and problem-solving skills? *(proud)*

▶ What do you think the rest of the school might learn about thinking and problem-solving skills?

UNIT 6

Cooperation

Cooperation is a skill that children begin to learn at a young age and will need to use throughout their lives on a daily basis. As the final Peacezone skill, cooperation derives from all the previous skills. In other words, to cooperate, one must use the Pledge for Peace and the skills of Trying Your Best, Self-Control, and Thinking and Problem Solving. It is important to point out to students how they are using all of these skills when they are cooperating with others.

When teaching cooperation, it is also important to stress that students can work with anyone. Make sure that students have the opportunity to cooperate with a variety of people, whether they are best friends or individuals with whom they are rarely in contact.

In school, students often learn how to cooperate with others by working in groups. You can use these opportunities to help students practice the skills needed to cooperate when solving a problem. Once students have internalized the skills needed to cooperate, they will be better able to work together peacefully when a problem arises with siblings at home, classmates at school, or friends on the playground.

You can remind students to cooperate in the following types of situations:

► Working on a group project

► Having a problem at recess

► Solving a problem with a classmate

► Making decisions as a class

► Deciding what game to play

► Deciding what to do after school

Daily Guidelines for Cooperation

► Remind students to follow the Pledge for Peace and use all the Peacezone skills when they cooperate.

► Provide positive reminders to cooperate when students are working in groups.

► Remind students that they can cooperate with anyone.

Introducing Cooperation

OBJECTIVE	Students will define and experience the skill of Cooperation.
MATERIALS	Cooperation poster (Appendix C)
VOCABULARY	**compromise** **huddle**
PROCEDURE	*Before teaching this lesson, hang the Cooperation poster in a prominent location in your classroom. Leave the poster up for future reference.*

Step 1 —— **Introduce the skill of Cooperation to the class.**

Cooperation

Cooperation is when I work well with others.

I cooperate to solve problems and resolve conflicts.

Cooperation helps me create peace.

Step 2 —— **Discuss how cooperation takes the Pledge for Peace and all of the Peacezone skills the students have learned so far.**

Discuss the following ideas:

► You must follow the Pledge for Peace: Treat others the way you want to be treated, respect diversity, use peaceful words, and have a positive attitude.

► You must use the skill of Trying Your Best when you work together.

► You must use the skill of Self-Control to follow the Pledge for Peace.

▶ You must use the skill of Thinking and Problem Solving to think of all the different ways that you can solve a problem.

STEP 3 —— **Give examples of how you, as an adult, use the skill of Cooperation in your life.**

For example, you might say you use this skill when you work with other teachers to decide what is best for students to learn.

STEP 4 —— **Give examples of how the students can use the skill of Cooperation at home, at school, and in the community.**

Share the idea that both children and adults must use this skill throughout the day. For example:

> *Home:* Cooperating with family members to redecorate a room
>
> *School:* Cooperating with other students in your reading group
>
> *Community:* Cooperating with others to plant a community garden

STEP 5 —— **Discuss ways others use cooperation and suggest how this applies to students.**

Explain that, to cooperate, both adults and children must be willing to work with all kinds of people. For example, on a baseball team, all of the players aren't best friends. They learn to cooperate and work together to be a successful team.

Let students know that when they cooperate with others, it does not always mean that they get what they want. People sometimes have to think of their second and third choices in order to cooperate. This is called **compromise,** which means that each person in the situation is willing to give something up to reach an agreement.

STEP 6 —— **Have the students experience the skill of Cooperation by playing the following game.**

Huddles

Purpose of the game

Students will learn the cooperation tool of the **huddle,** a partnership or small group of people who work together to solve problems. Students will also understand that cooperation takes the Pledge for Peace as well as all of the Peacezone skills.

How to play

Before you begin the game, remind students that, to cooperate, they must use all the skills they have learned so far, and let them know that they must cooperate to play the game.

Explain to the class that they are going to use huddles to cooperate with someone else:

> A huddle is a group of two or more people who cooperate together to solve a problem. When we are in a huddle, we stand facing each other and use our self-control to stay in our own space.

Have two students come to the front of the room to show the class what a huddle looks like. Remind students that when they cooperate they must be self-confident enough to work with anybody.

Ask students to find a student that they don't usually work with; then have the students form pairs. (You can also choose the pairs yourself.) Instruct the students to face their partners, and then encourage them to cooperate in their huddles to solve one of the following problems:

► You and your partner are in an ice cream shop, and you only have enough money for one scoop of ice cream. Unfortunately, when you get to the counter, the person serving the ice cream tells you that they are out of chocolate and vanilla. In your huddle, decide on one other flavor that you can share.

► You and your partner are together at recess. There is only one ball, and you both want to use it. In your huddle, cooperate and decide how you can solve the problem.

Tell the partners to cross their arms when they are finished. (This will let you know when they are done.)

Have each pair cooperate to share their answer with the class by saying it in unison. Remind the rest of the class to use their self-control to treat others the way they'd like to be treated and to be good listeners.

After the game is over, you can ask the following questions:

► What skills did you use to cooperate with your partner?

► Did you get your first choice when working on this problem? Do we always get our first choice when cooperating?

► When could you use huddles to solve problems at home and school?

To continue the game, suggest another situation appropriate for your class—for example, what you can do together on a Saturday afternoon that doesn't cost any money, what snack you would both enjoy, and what movie you would both like to watch.

STEP 7 —— **Do the Learning to Cooperate activity.**

Have students turn to page 36 in their Student Manuals (Learning to Cooperate) and tell them to circle the pictures of the people who are cooperating.

After they have done so, discuss their responses: What Peacezone skills are the people who are cooperating using?

First-grade extension: Ask for volunteers to act out one of these scenarios, using the Pledge for Peace and the Peacezone skills to cooperate.

LESSON 2

Reinforcing Cooperation

OBJECTIVE   Students will further explore the skill of Cooperation and apply it to their lives.

MATERIALS
- ▶ Copies of the Cooperation Puzzle activity (page 124)
- ▶ Construction paper, scissors, glue
- ▶ *For the game:* An assortment of building blocks
- ▶ *Optional:* Crayons or markers

PROCEDURE   *Cut the Cooperation Puzzle page into puzzle pieces for kindergartners. First graders can cut out their own puzzle pieces.*

STEP 1 —— **Review the skill of Cooperation from the previous lesson.**

Review the definition of cooperation on the Cooperation poster. Remind students that cooperation is a skill everyone uses and that they must use the Pledge for Peace and all their Peacezone skills when they cooperate.

Ask students what they learned from the game you played in the last lesson (Huddles).

STEP 2 —— **Reinforce the skill of Cooperation by playing the following game.**

Building Blocks of Cooperation

Purpose of the game

Students will work with others to practice cooperating in completing a task and will apply the skills needed to cooperate in their everyday lives.

How to play

Divide the class into groups of two or three. Remind students that they can work with anyone, not just friends.

Give each student four building blocks. The group will therefore have a total of eight to twelve building blocks. Keep eight building blocks for your own use.

Build a relatively simple structure with your blocks in a place that is visible to all students. Have students cooperate with their partner(s) to build the same structure: Students may share their ideas verbally, but they may not touch anyone else's blocks. Doing this will take a lot of self-control.

Circulate and help students cooperate as they build. Remind students to listen to one another, use their self-control, and think of all the different ways they can solve the problem together.

After the game is over, you can ask the following questions:

▶ Was it hard to cooperate with your partner(s)? Was it easier if you listened to each other, used your self-control, and tried your best to solve the problem together?

▶ What are some good things about working in a group?

▶ What are some other times when you have to cooperate with a group?

If you wish, repeat the activity by building another structure.

STEP 3 — **Discuss how cooperation helps people.**

Remind students about the community service activities they have done to help others and point out that they used the skill of Cooperation when they did them.

STEP 4 — **Do the Cooperation Puzzle activity.**

Have students turn to page 37 in their Student Manuals (Cooperation Puzzle) and explain that the people in the picture are talking about playing a game in which they must all cooperate.

Ask students what game they think the children in the circle are planning to play. *(any game requiring cooperation—four-square, jump rope, basketball or other team sports, and so forth)*

Follow the directions for your age group.

For kindergarten: Give each group of students a sheet of construction paper, some glue, and a set of puzzle pieces. Have them work together to reassemble the puzzle and glue it to the paper.

For first grade: Give each group of students a sheet of construction paper, scissors, some glue, and a copy of the Cooperation Puzzle activity. Have partners cooperate to cut out the puzzle pieces, reassemble the puzzle, and glue it to the paper.

When the students have finished, ask them how they cooperated on this task: What parts of the Pledge for Peace and Peacezone skills did they need to use to complete it?

If you wish to have the students color the Cooperation Puzzle on page 37 in their Student Manuals, distribute the crayons or markers and give them time to do so.

Cooperation Puzzle

Learning through Literature: Cooperation Stories

OBJECTIVE — Students will relate what they have learned about the skill of Cooperation to a story from the life of Louis D. Brown.

MATERIALS
- ▶ Crayons or markers
- ▶ Copies of the Cooperation Home Page (Appendix D)
- ▶ *Optional:* A copy of the story you choose to read to your class for students to keep or take home.
- ▶ *Optional:* Pictures of people in current events (from magazines and newspapers), glue

PROCEDURE

STEP 1 —— **Read the Louis D. Brown story about cooperation best suited to your class.**

The Remote's Control

—Recommended for kindergarten

Synopsis: Louis wants to watch his favorite television show, *Space Crusaders,* and his cousin Antonio wants to watch his favorite cartoon, *The Jetsons.* They argue so much that Louis's mother tells them that if they can't agree, neither one of them will be allowed to watch television. That's when the two boys cooperate to come up with a solution that they both can accept.

Read the story on pages 128–129.

After you have finished reading, discuss how the story relates to cooperation. Ask questions such as the following:

- ▶ Louis's mother says the boys need to cooperate and figure out a way to solve their problem. If you were Louis or Antonio, how would you have cooperated to solve this problem?

- ▶ Do you think Louis and Antonio's solution was a good one? Explain why or why not.

- ▶ When has there been a time when you had to cooperate? How did that work out?

Hector's Halloween Surprise

—Recommended for first grade

Synopsis: It's October 31st, and Hector's family doesn't have the money to buy him a Halloween costume. He's embarrassed by this and decides he won't go trick-or-treating with his friends. But when Louis and his other friends come to pick him up, they cooperate to figure out a way to make Hector a costume using things around his home.

Read the story on page 130.

After the story, have a discussion about how it relates to cooperation. Ask questions such as the following:

- ▶ At the beginning of the story, Hector is embarrassed because he can't afford to buy a Halloween costume. Can you think of a time when you cooperated with a family member or friend to make something rather than buy it?

- ▶ Because they saw that Hector was sad, Louis, Yen, and Emma all cooperated to help him find a solution to his problem. Do you think they came up with a good solution? Can you think of another solution?

STEP 2 —— **Do the Cooperation Role Model activity.**

Have the class turn to page 38 in their Student Manuals (Cooperation Role Model). Have students choose a person in current events who is a role model for cooperation, and then have them draw a picture of that person in the frame. (If magazine or newspaper pictures of these individuals are available, the students can glue these to the page.)

First-grade extension: On the lines provided, have students write down the reasons they chose this person as their cooperation role model. Give assistance as needed.

S<small>TEP</small> 3 —— **Assign the Cooperation Home Page.**

Give students a copy of the Cooperation Home Page to share with their parents or caregivers.

PEACEZONE

The Remote's Control

Blue Telusma

Hi! My name is Louis, and in a couple of minutes my favorite show, *Space Crusaders,* will be coming on television. I can't wait to watch it. I have my popcorn and my soda all ready. I cleaned up my room like my mom asked, and I even have on the Space Crusaders cape that my dad bought me for Christmas last year.

"Up, up, and away!" the announcer says. "It's time for the Space Crusaders!"

The second I hear those words, I jump up and do the special Space Crusaders salute.

"What are you doing?" my cousin Antonio asks, as he walks into the living room.

"I'm doing the Crusader salute," I reply. "You wanna watch it with me?"

"Aw, man, you still like that silly show?" Antonio teases, grabbing the remote out of my hand. "Let's watch *The Jetsons* instead. That's what all the cool kids watch now."

And, just like that, he changes the channel. I am so mad, I can't believe it. How dare he walk into my house and turn off my show!

"Give that back, Antonio," I scream.

"No," he yells back, jumping off the couch with the remote still in his hand.

With my Space Crusaders cape flapping behind me, I run after him and leap on his back to stop him from running away.

"Get off me, Louis. I want to watch *The Jetsons.*"

"Well, that's too bad. Change it back—I'm missing my show!"

"Hey, what's going on here?" my mom yells, coming into the room. "Boys, use your self-control and get off each other right now!" Uh-oh. I can tell she's mad.

"Are you two fighting over the TV again?"

We nod.

Peacezone: A Program for Teaching Social Literacy—Teacher's Guide (Grades K–1)
Copyright © 2005 by the authors. Champaign, Illinois: Research Press (800) 519–2707.

The Remote's Control *(continued)*

"Well, that's it. If the two of you can't cooperate, no one will be able to watch television again for the rest of the week," Mom warns as she storms out of the room with the remote in her hand.

"What's cooperate?" Antonio asks, looking confused.

"It means she wants us to work together to solve our problem."

"How are we supposed to do that?"

"How about we flip a coin?" I suggest.

"Nah. That wouldn't be fair because only one of us would win," Antonio points out. "We need to think of something else," he says, scratching his head.

After a couple of seconds, his eyes light up, and I know he has come up with something good.

"Hey, I have an idea. How about we split up the days?"

"What do you mean, split up the days?" I ask.

"You could watch your show one day, and then I'd get to watch my show the next day. That way, we'd both be happy, and we wouldn't have to fight over the remote anymore."

"That's a great idea!" I say, finally smiling again. "There's just one thing, though."

"What's that?" Antonio asks.

"Since I already have my cape on, can today be my turn?"

"Sure," he says, laughing.

And for the rest of the hour, we sit on the couch and watch *Space Crusaders* together.

Hector's Halloween Surprise

Blue Telusma

"Trick or treat!"

When I opened the door, my friends Louis, Yen, and Emma were all on my doorstep in their Halloween costumes.

"Hey, Hector! Where's your costume?" Emma asked, looking me up and down. "Aren't you going trick-or-treating with us?"

"No, I can't go," I answered, disappointed.

"Why not?" Louis asked, as I let them in.

"Because, before Nana died, she used to make all my costumes. And now that she's gone, Dad says we can't afford to buy one from the store."

Talking about my Nana's being gone always made me sad. Everything changed after she died. And my not being able to go trick-or-treating with my friends was just another example of that change.

"You don't need money to get a costume," Yen said, seeing how sad I had become.

"What do you mean, I don't need money?"

"Well, look at me. I made mine all by myself, and it didn't cost me anything. I just put on some black tights and a black turtleneck, drew some whiskers with my mom's makeup pencil, and put on my Josey and the Pussycats fuzzy ears, and ta da! Now I'm Cat Woman!"

Yen had a point. She was Cat Woman.

"That's really cool. But I don't know how to do that."

"It's okay. We'll help you."

For about five minutes, my friends and I all ran around my house looking for things to use for a costume. Mom gave me an old white sheet, and Louis found some arts and crafts supplies in my room.

Because everyone cooperated and worked together, I was soon standing in the living room showing off my new Casper the Friendly Ghost costume. It wasn't as nice as the costumes Nana used to make for me, but it was better than nothing. And I could go trick-or-treating!

Hector's Halloween Surprise *(continued)*

My friends had really come through for me when I needed them the most. And because of that, I ended up having the best Halloween ever. I was proud of myself, and I think Nana would have been proud, too.

Community Service Learning: Helping Hands

OBJECTIVE   Students will apply the skill of Cooperation as they complete a community service project.

MATERIALS   Construction paper, pencils, scissors, tape

VOCABULARY   **helping hand**

PROCEDURE

STEP 1 —— **Remind students of the meaning of *community* and *community service*.**

Ask students to tell you the meaning of the words *community* (a group of people who work together) and *community service* (things we do to give to our community).

STEP 2 —— **Introduce the project.**

Explain that to give someone a **helping hand** means that you give someone else help when the person needs it. Ask questions like the following:

▶ How have you seen people lend a helping hand to one another?

▶ When have you lent a helping hand to someone else?

Let students know that they will be making "helping hands" as a community service project.

STEP 3 —— **Do the project.**

Divide students into huddles of two or three. Give these groups enough sheets of construction paper, pencils, and scissors to go around.

Ask students to cooperate in their groups to trace one another's palm prints on the construction paper. (Students should trace both hands.)

After the students have traced their hands, ask questions such as the following:

► How did it feel to help someone out in your group?

► How did it feel to be helped?

► Could we do this activity on our own, without help?

Have students cut out their own hand tracings from the construction paper. (Give assistance as needed.)

STEP 4 —— **Ask students for suggestions about how they can lend a helping hand in the classroom.**

Have students choose two ways (one for each hand) that they are going to lend a helping hand in the classroom. For example,

Give students assistance as needed to write their choices on their hand tracings.

STEP 5 —— **Present the project.**

Tape the helping hands on the classroom walls. Refer to the helping hands to remind the students to help out as needed.

STEP 6 —— **Take time to reflect.**

After the activity is completed, make sure to take the time to have the students reflect on the project. You can ask the following questions:

General Questions

► What was doing this project like for you?

► Which part of the project did you like the least? The most?

► What parts of the Pledge for Peace and Peacezone skills did you use while you were doing this project?

Responses to this question can include any and all of the aspects of the Pledge for Peace and the skills of Trying Your Best, Self-Control, Thinking and Problem Solving, and Cooperating.

► How did you feel when you finished the project?

As a culmination of the Peacezone program, brainstorm how the class can lend a helping hand to the community. With the students' input, develop a community service project to help a group or organization in the community.

As you plan and execute your effort, review and reinforce the Pledge for Peace and the Peacezone skills the students have learned.

Specific Questions

► How has doing this project shown the importance of helping out?

► What are some ways you lend a helping hand at home?

► What could we do throughout the school to lend a helping hand?

Program Theory and Evaluation

PROGRAM THEORY

The Peacezone curriculum incorporates both the intrapersonal intelligences that help children manage their own feelings and the interpersonal intelligences that help children get along with others and care for the world around them. These concepts help children become "emotionally literate" and develop the skills needed to resist risk-taking behavior.

The Peacezone program is informed by the ecological model for health promotion (McElroy, 1988). The ecological model, which implies a reciprocal relationship between the individual and the environment, views health promotion strategies as based upon five levels, in which change in behavior is determined by (1) characteristics of the individual; (2) interpersonal processes (i.e., family and peers); (3) institutional factors; (4) community factors; and (5) public policy. Peacezone operates at all five levels to change attitudes, beliefs, and behaviors; provide and develop skills; and improve school climate. The program is informed by social learning theory (Bandura, 1977, 1989) and addresses its four major components by (1) teaching and demonstrating the consequences of risk-taking behavior through facilitated, age-appropriate classroom discussions and activities; (2) teaching students the major components of the Peacezone program; (3) providing a safe environment within which to practice new decision-making and communication skills with positive reinforcement; and (4) offering students the opportunity to make a commitment to prevent violence on an individual and environmental level.

The Peacezone program is predicated upon the belief that emotional and social skills must be incorporated into all primary school curricula. Although teaching emotional and social skills as an integral part of a social skills curriculum is a comparatively new idea, others have advanced the theory that developing the emotional domain can enhance personal adjustment and resiliency throughout life (e.g., Gardner, 1983; Goleman, 1995). Several researchers have

135

advanced the theory that cultivation of the emotional domain can enhance one's personal adjustment and resiliency throughout life. Howard Gardner (1983) has played a major role in helping educators make this link between the cognitive and affective domains. In his book *Frames of Mind,* he identifies two competencies, or intelligences, which form the basis of the concept of social and emotional literacy necessary for effective social interaction. Recent research has supported the importance of emotional skills such as responsibility, impulse control, empathy, and caring over skills of intelligence, specifically IQ. Documenting a fifteen-year decline, an increase in "emotional illiteracy" that cuts across racial and class boundaries, Goleman (1995) proscribes the need for schools to teach self-control, persistence, and zeal—qualities that are far more important to safety and civility than being the class valedictorian or a Rhodes Scholar. The Peacezone program accomplishes what Gardner and his colleagues recommend: emotional and social skills integrated into daily curricula.

PROGRAM EVALUATION

The U.S. Department of Education funded the Harvard School of Public Health, Louis D. Brown Peace Institute, and Lesson One Company to create, pilot, and evaluate the Peacezone program. In Phase 1 (1998–2001), Peacezone was developed and piloted in one elementary school. After three years of demonstrated effectiveness, the partnering groups were awarded Phase 2 (2001–2003) funding for implementation and evaluation in three intervention and control schools. Peacezone was created with a formative evaluation process and evaluated using pretest and posttest surveys, which were administered to students in Grades 3–5. Phase 2 was completed in September 2003.

In today's classroom, teachers and their students face multiple demands on their time. Any time away from academic subjects must be time well spent. To ensure that the time you and your students invest in the Peacezone program will be valuable, we spent four years evaluating the program. The results were quite positive:

▶ Students participating in the Peacezone program improved their prosocial behaviors, and the overall school climate also improved (Year 3).

▶ Students receiving instruction through the Peacezone program reported an increase in the level of classmates' prosocial behavior that was greater than the increase reported by students in a school with a similar student population that did not receive Peacezone instruction (i.e., a control school).

The most significant change was for those students who scored very low (few prosocial and many antisocial behaviors) during the first survey administration (before the Peacezone program was implemented) and those who reported higher levels of exposure to community violence (Year 3 pretest to posttest: t = -2.18, p = .031; Year 2 pretest to Year 3 posttest: (t = -1.94, p > .050).

Both boys and girls participating in the Peacezone program reported that they were victimized significantly less after the Peacezone program was implemented in their school (initial results, Year 4: boys, t = 1.645, p = .1; girls, t = 2.173, p = .03). In addition, boys in the Peacezone schools reported perpetrating significantly less violence against other children in school (t = 1.612, p = .1).

Survey results before the Peacezone program began and results after the program was implemented showed that both boys and girls experienced extremely significant reductions in depression (boys, t = 5.611, p < .001; girls, t = 7.212, p < .001). Girls who witnessed or had been victimized through violence in the community were less likely after participating in the Peacezone program to report being depressed than they were prior to Peacezone implementation.

REFERENCES   Bandura, A. (1977). *Social learning theory.* Englewood Cliffs, NJ: Prentice-Hall.

Bandura, A. (1989). Regulation of cognitive processes through perceived self-efficacy. *Developmental Psychology, 25*(5), 729–735.

Bandura, A., Valentine, E. R., Nesdale, A. R., Farr, R., Goodnow, J. J., Lloyd, B., & Duveen, G. (1989). Recent advances in social psychology: An international perspective. In J. P. Forgas, J. Innes, J. Michael et al. (Eds.), *Social cognition* (pp. 127–188). Amsterdam: North-Holland.

Gardner, H. (1983). *Frames of mind: The theory of multiple intelligences.* New York: Basic Books.

Goleman, D. P. (1995). *Emotional intelligence: Why it can matter more than IQ for character, health and lifelong achievement.* New York: Bantam.

McElroy, K. (1988). An ecological perspective on health promotion programs. *Health Education Quarterly, 15,* 351–377.

Louis D. Brown Story

(Adult Version)

Nancy O'Keefe Bolick

Wrong Place, Wrong Time?

Louis David Brown dreamed on a wide screen. He was fifteen and a tenth grader at West Roxbury High School in the fall of 1993, and he'd already decided he was going places. College was high on his agenda, then graduate school, where he intended to earn a doctoral degree in aerodynamic engineering. But his long-term goal, the one he talked about a lot with his family and friends, was to become the first black—and the youngest ever—president of the United States.

So chances are you might have heard about Louis in the year 2015 or so, when he would have been in his mid-thirties and maybe living in the White House. As a teenager, he was already working toward the goals he set for himself, earning good grades in school and beginning to investigate the problem of crime, violence, and racism that he could see in Dorchester, Massachusetts, where he'd lived his whole life. The first step to learning to govern a country, he believed, was to learn about the problems in your own community and try to help solve them.

But as big as they were, and as hard as he pursued them, Louis's dreams were shattered just as he was starting to firm them up. On December 20, 1993, on his way to the Christmas party of the group he'd just joined, Teens Against Gang Violence, Louis was killed. He was an innocent victim, caught in a gunfight on the corner of Geneva Avenue and Tonawanda Street, near Fields Corner in Dorchester, just as he was about to enter the subway ramp to catch a train to Mattapan Square. It was the middle of a winter afternoon, five days before Christmas.

In trying to figure out why the tragedy happened, some people lamented that Louis was just caught in the wrong place at the wrong time. But his cousin, Antonio Thompson, who was two years younger than Louis and one of his best friends, says that simply isn't so. Antonio remembers his aunt saying that you see lots of signs that say "No Parking" or "No Stopping," but you never see a sign that says "Do Not Walk on Geneva Avenue at Around

3:15 in the Afternoon Because There Will Be a Gang Shootout." If you did, then you'd be in the wrong place at the wrong time.

The irony of Louis's death is that he had tried to insulate himself from the dangers on the streets. He spent most of his time at home, up in his third-floor room, playing video games, watching TV, dunking a basketball in a laundry bag he'd hung on a door, reading, doing his homework, and listening to rap and rhythm and blues. Friends like Anthony Potter and his cousin Antonio would hang out there with him for hours at a time. His house on Dahlgren Street was the place friends and relatives liked to congregate.

Louis's parents, Joseph and Clementina (Tina) Chéry, tried to protect their son from the violence they knew existed in their neighborhood, as it does all over this country. They drove him everywhere, insisted on tight curfews when he was out with his friends, and created a strong, supportive home atmosphere for him, his five-year-old sister, Alexandra, and his two-year-old brother, Allen. But since his death, his parents wonder if there was anything else they could have done.

They say they didn't push him to stay home, but they didn't encourage him to get out that much either. His mother believes Louis was aware of what was going on out on the streets and he wasn't quite prepared to deal with it. He'd hint at the problems, but he wouldn't talk a lot about them.

Joseph Chéry could also see that his son was wary of people in the neighborhood. In the summertime, kids would come down the street and put up a basketball hoop. The closest Louis would be to those games was on the porch, watching. He stayed in the house as much as he could.

It was obvious to Louis that things had changed in his neighborhood, where he'd lived his whole life. When he was a little boy, there were young families and lots of little kids around, and all the children played together. But then the people who owned the houses began to move away. They were replaced by renters, and Louis and his family didn't get to know them because they came and went so quickly. There were no kids to hang out with.

Since Louis's killing, his father has begun to think about what it means to be part of a community where violence is common. To him, Louis's death proved that even innocent people die in violent crimes, even when they don't think they'll be affected. After spending so much time protecting his family only to see his eldest child killed in a random act, he now asks himself why. He wonders if he tried too hard to keep Louis from the dangers that were all around.

"We realized when Louis was killed that part of the problem can be staying home, closing the window, or refusing to call 911. Part of the solution is to get involved," Joseph Chéry says.

First Black President

Getting involved is just what Louis was beginning to do before he died. Another cousin, Antoinette "Tonie" Johnson, who called Louis "Lulu" and who was nearly a sister to him from the time they were little kids, had joined a group called Teens Against Gang Violence and asked Louis if he'd like to come to a meeting to see what it was all about. His parents were surprised that he went with Tonie, and even more surprised that he came home so excited about the group. They used to urge Louis to get involved in activities with kids his age, but he was never interested. Even when they signed him up for karate, when he was eight, he'd hide in the bathtub when it was time to go to practice. So they were amazed when Louis decided on his own to go to the meeting with Tonie and then to join the group. And they saw that after he did, he became more talkative and happier. At home, he related what they discussed at the meetings all the time.

Ulric Johnson started Teens Against Gang Violence in 1990 as a way of making young people aware of the problems in their neighborhoods so they could get involved and become part of the solution. Contrary to what some people think, the group is not a haven for ex–gang members. It's a place for teenagers who view peace and justice as means of reducing violence. Johnson met Louis when Tonie took him to that first meeting.

Johnson remembers when Louis showed up, a tall, good-looking kid in headphones and thin-framed glasses who quickly entered the group discussion. The talk turned to the building blocks of Teens Against Gang Violence. They are *color,* which means appreciation of your roots; *class,* how you use your own power; *character,* appreciating yourself as an individual; and *community,* having pride in where you live. When group members were asked what they liked about themselves, Louis said he was a handsome, intelligent, young black male, and from that time on he joked around with the other members, sang rap, and generally fit right in. When Johnson spoke to the group about gang violence, homicide, and drugs in the black community, Louis listened intently. Often Louis used to say, "I want the kids I went to school with, the kids from my community, to be active in my government. However, if things don't change, I'll be alone in the White House because by the time I become president my peers will all be doped up, in jail, or dead."

Louis's parents remember Louis's telling them that the Teens Against Gang Violence was part of a larger effort to have young people change their ways, and they'd never seen him so excited about anything. He was impressed that kids his age felt the same way he did and were articulating it. They had something to offer, and other kids and adults were listening. His father says that just blew Louis's mind.

His friends and family describe Louis as a basically quiet, nondemonstrative kid who listened and paid attention at home and at school. He attended the John Marshall School from kindergarten through grade 3; the Richard Murphy School for grades 4 and 5; and the Martin Luther King, Jr., School for grades 6 through 8. He spent a short time at Jeremiah Burke High School while he was waiting for a place to open up at West Roxbury High School.

Joan Doherty, Louis's fifth-grade teacher at the Murphy School, remembers him as a wonderful boy with a bright future. He'd been chosen for an advanced-work class based on his reading and math test scores, and he fit in beautifully with the group of talented students. Doherty remembers Louis as a special kid—warm, personable, and polite—a boy who was always kind to others, who told the truth, who had a curious mind and wanted to learn and do well. She says he always had a smile on his face.

But even though Louis was a bright, capable student, like most kids, he didn't always do his homework, and Doherty would have to call his parents about that. Louis wasn't a saint, she remembers, but she says he was pretty close to it, and what happened to him should never have happened.

Louis's father recalls a seventh-grade project that showed in a very visual way how focused and determined his son was becoming. That year at the Martin Luther King, Jr., School, a teacher asked students to consider the kind of life they imagined for themselves in the future. Louis created a poster with a picture of the Huxtable family (from TV's *Bill Cosby Show)* and said that his idol was President George H. W. Bush and that he intended to get his Ph.D. in aerodynamics.

But although Louis was smart, when he was younger he wasn't one to work hard. Like many teenagers who want to excel, he struggled with his image in school. His parents would check his homework regularly, but then they'd frequently get notes from teachers saying he'd failed to turn in some assignments. While Louis would claim he'd forgotten or lost his homework, his mother would later find it stashed in his backpack, a book, or a pocket.

It was only later that they realized the problem had to do with the peer culture at school. Louis's peers thought it wasn't cool for kids to be smart. And Louis wanted to be a kid. So he'd do the work he was responsible for, but he'd stay true to the teen spirit of school by not turning in his homework.

Louis also always thought he'd be famous some day, so he felt there was no point in working too hard for it because it was going to happen anyway. His parents' biggest fear was that he'd become lazy. They could see he wasn't putting in much effort. That allowed him to slide by in school for a while, but eventually his grades started to slip.

His parents got him out of that spiral when they realized how strong his desire was to become president. They pushed and pushed, making references to his behavior and that of George Bush and reminding him how the president got to be where he is, which was through plenty of hard work. Imagine Bush writing his State of the Union address, stashing it in a drawer, and then appearing before Congress without the text, they'd tell Louis. That seemed to make Louis understand that excellence involved effort. From that point on, his school performance picked up.

At West Roxbury High, Louis was enrolled in honors classes and was thinking of trying out for the basketball and football teams. He told his cousin Tonie he was also considering the football team because his ex-girlfriend's ex-boyfriend played for another school and, he said, he couldn't wait to meet him on the field. Tonie says all the girls urged him to play basketball.

Long-Long

Louis lived most of his life in his third-floor bedroom, surrounded by his stuff and by stacks of books that he read for pleasure and to fulfill school assignments. His reading was eclectic and included these titles: *Charlie and the Chocolate Factory; Oprah, To Be Popular or Smart; The Black Peer Group; To Kill a Mockingbird; The Book of Presidents; I Am Third (the story of Brian Piccolo and Gale Sayers); The Adventures of Huck Finn;* and *The Lexicon Universal Encyclopedia.* But he also loved comic books like *Archie* and *The Marvels,* and he collected *TV Week.*

One of the qualities Louis's family and friends miss now that he's gone is his sense of humor. His friends in Teens against Gang Violence remember him as always laughing, telling jokes, and singing. And he liked to tease his parents, too.

A couple of times Louis's parents let him go into town with his friends. They'd leave at about ten in the morning, and he had strict orders to be home at six o'clock. His mother would tell him not to get on the train at six or call her at six but be home by six. The last time they went, he called to say they were really sorry, but they'd gotten sidetracked and they'd be late. She just told him to get on the train. Then two minutes later they walked in the house—they'd called from the corner store. His mother commented on the quick trip and Louis said, "Oh, yeah, I'm a responsible child." He was always playing around like that.

Louis was also a peaceful young man who did what he was asked at home, although he almost resented the fact that his parents were so reasonable in their requests. His mother says he thought of them as weird parents because they didn't demand things from him, didn't say, "Do this, do that, or else." They always asked him politely to do things around the house. She remembers one night when she asked him to clean up.

The family was sitting around after dinner, and Mrs. Chéry asked Louis to please do the dishes. He agreed—he'd rather wash dishes than clean his room—but he did the dishes in his own special way. He sat on a stool, put his feet on a chair, and turned on the TV. It took him three hours to wash a few plates. When he finished, he asked his parents why they weren't like other parents who ordered their kids around without any discussion. That would give him something to rebel against, he said. Because they always asked him nicely, he felt he didn't have much choice but to do what he was asked.

If Louis thought his parents were different from the norm, his parents thought he was different from other kids. He didn't demand lots of things like some teenagers tend to do, and he looked out for his younger sister and brother. At Christmas, for example, he knew what he wanted from his parents, his aunts, and his grandmother, and he'd only ask for one thing from each of them.

"Louis may have had his little problems, like anyone," says his cousin Antonio. Antonio remembers when he was in fourth grade and going through a "Save the Environment" phase. One day he was at Louis's house, and he started nagging Louis about being so messy and kept telling him to pick up the stuff he'd dumped all over the floor. Louis said he didn't have to if he didn't want to, so when he left the room, Antonio just threw it all out the third-floor window. Then he got scared, started to cry, and left before Louis came back. The next day Louis was still mad, but he talked to Antonio again. He wasn't the kind of kid to hold a grudge.

"But if you really think about it, Louis was the perfect kid to Tina and Joe. He was going to be president, and I was going to be vice president, even though he was a conservative Republican and I'm a Democrat," Antonio says.

Louis's parents also took pride in his relationships with his younger siblings. One evening when the family was having dinner at a restaurant, it became clear that he was doing his part to educate them. Alexandra started talking while she was eating, and Mrs. Chéry was about to correct her when Louis jumped in and told his sister not to talk while her mouth was full because it was improper and she could choke. Later she was pointing to someone in the restaurant, and he told her that wasn't polite. Mrs. Chéry told Louis she was impressed that he'd actually been listening to the things she had tried to teach him, and, with his habitual smile, he told her that of course he had, but he couldn't say so because that would give her a big head.

Alexandra was only four when her big brother was killed, but she prays every day for Louis. She remembers that he was lots of fun and that she misses his playing "X-Man" with her, reading, and coloring. Little Allen was less than a year old when Louis died, so he'll have to rely on pictures and his family's stories to remember the brother he never really knew.

Alexandra also remembers how much Louis liked to eat. He enjoyed rice, chicken, and beans, she says, but his favorite was Chinese food. The best traveled path in the Chéry household was the one Louis would take from his room or the den's couch to the refrigerator. He used to eat everything he could get his hands on.

Everyone in Louis's extended family thought he was special, not just because he was a great kid. He was the first in the family to be born in the United States (Louis's mother is from Honduras, his father from Haiti), the first boy, and the first grandchild. Louis's aunt, Julia Thompson, remembers him as the cutest little thing she'd ever seen when he was born, but she thought his head was rather long, so she nicknamed him "Long-Long." She never called him Louis unless she was mad at him, and he called her "Etta."

When Louis was little, Julia would take him and Antonio out for Chinese food every other Sunday. That was before she learned to drive, so she'd take them on the subway, and they'd try different places in Chinatown every time. That's probably how Louis became hooked on Chinese food.

A Guiding Light

The people who loved Louis struggled with some guilt over his death, even though they knew there was nothing they could have done to prevent it. His cousin Tonie had offered to pick him up on her way to the party, but he refused, saying she was always late and he wanted to be on time. Ulric Johnson, who used to encourage group members to be punctual, has had to fight to overcome the guilt that Louis left home early to get to the group's Christmas party on time. If we'd scheduled it on a different day or at a different time, he might not have died, Johnson thinks.

Louis's Aunt Julia was at home sick the day of the shooting, so she couldn't drive him. And although his mother had offered to take him, her license had just expired, and Louis didn't want her to get into trouble if she got stopped by the police. He told her he'd take the subway.

But he made it only as far as the ramp to the subway, just a few blocks from his home, before he was gunned down. Police suspect the killers were gang members involved in a drug deal. Louis's death touched people in Boston and around the country with a concern that crossed cultural and class lines. Ulric Johnson explains it this way: Johnson says lots of parents believe they're doing their best to protect their kids. But this incident resonated with a lot of people. You could describe Louis as an honor student going to a meeting and not mention color and it could be any kid anywhere in the country.

The perception is that areas like Dorchester and Roxbury and Mattapan are drastically unsafe places to live. Yes, there are problems in these communities, just as there are anywhere else, and those problems are forcing lots of people to move out in favor of places like Randolph and Brockton. But Johnson tries to show teenagers the good parts of their communities and explain why people shouldn't simply move out.

The reality is that all black kids in Roxbury and Dorchester and Mattapan are not in gangs. Because a kid lives in the 'hood, it doesn't automatically mean he's in a gang. And kids are also part of the solution, not just part of the problem.

But some people called for Ulric Johnson to disband Teens Against Gang Violence after Louis's death, saying he was killed because he was a member of a gang and that the program was putting kids at risk. It's just the opposite, Johnson says. Those kids were never in gangs. Teens against Gang Violence does its part by trying to address stereotypes. There are gangs everywhere. They may not be labeled gangs, but they participate in violent acts. There are guns in good communities, too, and those are the kinds of issues the group tries to discuss at conferences and in presentations to groups.

Members not only rejected the idea of disbanding Teens Against Gang Violence, they were even more committed to being good role models and to pointing out that communities need to work for causes like these: creating youth centers and more youth programs, hiring street workers, passing tougher gun-control laws, and improving the police department's response to crime. They find inspiration in Louis D. Brown.

Louis's cousin Tonie isn't sure what he might have accomplished in the group, but she does know he was a good addition and something of a guiding light for the others. She says that all of the kids in the group are smart, even though it might not be obvious from some of the grades they get. Louis's openness was refreshing. He came in and said he was a really good-looking black male and a funny guy, and by doing that he allowed the rest of them to loosen up, showing them they could say what they wanted to without people taking it the wrong way. And he got good grades. That was a big influence on the group. Even afterwards, many of them have done better in school.

Antonio Thompson was probably closer to Louis than anyone. A year after Louis's death, Antonio received his first report card that sparkled with all *A*s. He says he thinks about his cousin every day, that there's a history to everything in his house that's connected to Louis.

Louis Brown's brain died the instant a bullet tore into his head in the middle of a winter afternoon. This bullet was followed by another to his side, but machines at Boston City Hospital kept him alive for another thirteen hours. Louis's killers still haven't been caught. Although his mother says she still has days when she wants to scream and lash out at someone, anyone, to ease the pain, both Chérys have turned their personal tragedy into something positive for the whole community. They created The Louis D. Brown Peace Institute to advance the causes of peace and nonviolence. And this curriculum came about with their help and hard work. Louis D. Brown wasn't a saint, as his teacher said, or a superhero. He was a regular kid who wore baggy pants, sweaters, and sneakers. He listened to rap and joked around with his friends. He worked hard in school and had ambitions for himself and for others in his community. He was like so many of you, a good kid with a future waiting for him.

We'll never know if Louis could have made it to the White House, whether he'd have continued to be interested in aerodynamics, or if he'd have returned to Dorchester to work for peace. What is evident is that his life has become the inspiration for others to think about violence and ways to prevent it, and his memory continues to remind those who knew him to do well, to be kind, to try to make a difference.

Peacezone Posters

Louis D. Brown

Louis was a fifteen-year-old peace-maker from Dorchester, Massachusetts, who worried about violence in his community. He promoted peace by performing community service. He spoke to his peers about the dangers of guns and drugs. Louis dreamed of becoming the first black president of the United States. Louis's dream for peace has inspired the Peacezone program.

You are not too young to make peace. Start now!

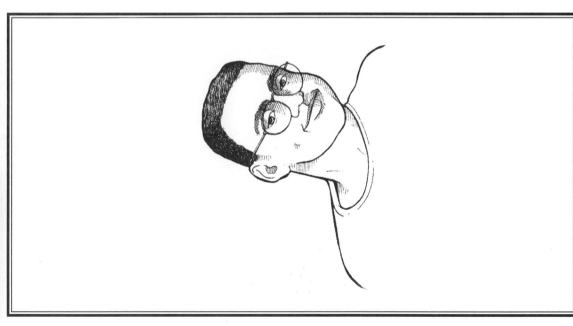

Peacezone: A Program for Teaching Social Literacy—Teacher's Guide (Grades K–1)
Copyright © 2005 by the authors. Champaign, Illinois: Research Press (800) 519–2707.

Pledge for Peace

▲ I will treat others the way I want to be treated.

Caring about others makes me and those around me feel good. Pushing, fighting, bullying, name-calling, and treating others badly hurts them and me.

▲ I will respect the diversity of all people.

Whether we are the same or different on the outside, it is the person we are on the inside that counts.

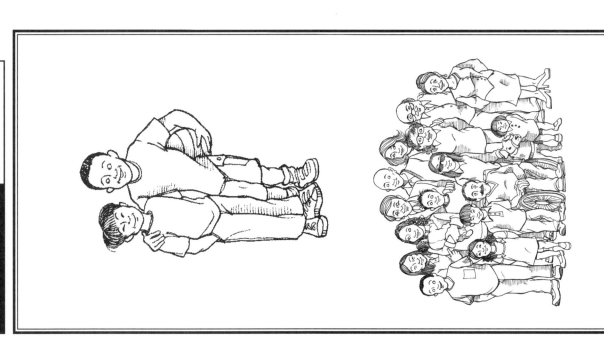

PEACE ZONE

▲ I will use peaceful words.

Using words that are kind and friendly will help me create a peaceful home, school, and community.

▲ I will have a positive attitude.

Thinking and believing "I can" instead of "I can't" helps me be successful in life.

Peacezone: A Program for Teaching Social Literacy—Teacher's Guide (Grades K–1)
Copyright © 2005 by the authors. Champaign, Illinois: Research Press (800) 519–2707.

Trying Your Best

▲ I will try my best.

▲ Even when I make mistakes, I learn from them.

▲ The most important thing is to keep trying.

▲ When I try my best, I get a proud, happy feeling called self-confidence.

Peacezone: A Program for Teaching Social Literacy—Teacher's Guide (Grades K–1)
Copyright © 2005 by the authors. Champaign, Illinois: Research Press (800) 519–2707.

Self-Control

▲ Self-control is when I am in charge of what I do and what I say.

▲ I use my self-control to listen and follow directions.

▲ Using self-control helps me not do things that may be harmful to myself and others.

▲ Self-control helps me stay safe, be successful, and create peace.

Peacezone: A Program for Teaching Social Literacy—Teacher's Guide (Grades 4–5)
Copyright © 2005 by the authors. Champaign, Illinois: Research Press (800) 519–2707.

Self-Control Time

Self-Control Time is a fun breathing exercise to help me calm down, focus, and get my self-control back.

Steps

1. Sit comfortably with your back against the chair.

2. Place your feet flat on the floor in front of you.

3. Place your hands so they are extended gently on your lap.

4. Relax your shoulders so the muscles around them are not tight or tense.

5. Breathe deeply through your nose and exhale through your mouth.

6. Close your eyelids lightly and focus on your breathing.

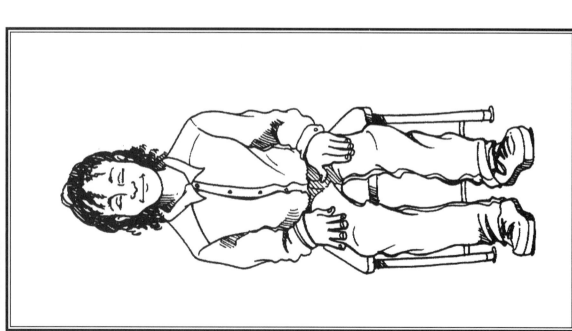

PEACEZONE

156

Peacezone: A Program for Teaching Social Literacy—Teacher's Guide (Grades 4–5)
Copyright © 2005 by the authors. Champaign, Illinois: Research Press (800) 519–2707.

Thinking and Problem Solving

▲ Thinking is when I come up with as many ideas as I can.

▲ Problem solving is when I think in order to find the solution to a problem.

▲ I keep thinking until I solve the problem. I don't give up.

▲ Thinking and problem solving help me find ways to create peace.

157

Peacezone: A Program for Teaching Social Literacy—Teacher's Guide (Grades 4–5)
Copyright © 2005 by the authors. Champaign, Illinois: Research Press (800) 519–2707.

Five Steps of Thinking and Problem Solving

STEP 1: What is the problem?

STEP 2: What are my choices?

STEP 3: What are the consequences of my choices? (What could happen?)

STEP 4: Make a choice.

STEP 5: How did I do?

158

Peacezone: A Program for Teaching Social Literacy—Teacher's Guide (Grades 4–5)
Copyright © 2005 by the authors. Champaign, Illinois: Research Press (800) 519–2707.

Cooperation

▲ Cooperation is when I work well with others.

▲ I cooperate to solve problems and resolve conflicts.

▲ Cooperation helps me create peace.

Peacezone: A Program for Teaching Social Literacy—Teacher's Guide (Grades 4–5)
Copyright © 2005 by the authors. Champaign, Illinois: Research Press (800) 519–2707.

Peacezone Home Pages

Louis D. Brown Home Page

Welcome to the Peacezone program! Throughout the year, we will be learning about Louis D. Brown and how his peacemaking skills can help our children be safe and reach their full potential.

Louis D. Brown was a fifteen-year-old peacemaker from Dorchester, Massachusetts, who was worried about the effect of violence on his community. He dreamed of becoming the first black president of the United States. Louis was the innocent victim of a gang shooting in 1993. The skills taught in the Peacezone program were important to Louis because he wanted all children to be safe and achieve their dreams.

Pledge for Peace Home Page

Please hang this page on your refrigerator door and try using the Pledge for Peace in your home.

Your children are doing a great job with the Peacezone program. They are learning life skills that will help them with their academics, get along with others, and believe in themselves. As a school, we have made a **Pledge for Peace.** We begin each day by reciting and sharing about this pledge.

Pledge for Peace

▶ **I will treat others the way I want to be treated.**

Caring about others makes me and those around me feel good. Pushing, fighting, bullying, name-calling, and treating others badly hurts them and me.

▶ **I will respect the diversity of all people.**

Whether we are the same or different on the outside, it's the person we are on the inside that counts.

▶ **I will use peaceful words.**

Using words that are kind and friendly will help me create a peaceful home, school, and community.

▶ **I will have a positive attitude.**

Thinking and believing "I can" instead of "I can't" helps me be successful in life.

On the back of this page, work together with your child to list all the different times and places you and your child use the Pledge for Peace.

PEACE ZONE

Trying Your Best Home Page

Please hang this page on your refrigerator door and try using the skill of Trying Your Best in your home.

Together, we are continuing to create a "peace zone" at your child's school. We are now talking about the skill of **Trying Your Best.** We have talked about how it is okay to make mistakes as long as we learn from them. We have also talked about how trying our best makes us feel proud and self-confident.

Please share with your child how you try your best and refer to this skill throughout the day.

Trying Your Best

▶ **I will try my best.**

▶ **Even when I make mistakes, I learn from them.**

▶ **The most important thing is to keep trying.**

▶ **When I try my best, I get a proud, happy feeling called self-confidence.**

With your child, please answer the following questions and have fun talking about trying your best!

1. Share a time when you made a mistake and how you learned from the mistake you made.

2. With your child, list all the different times you and your child have tried your best.

   _____   _____

   _____   _____

   _____   _____

   _____   _____

3. Discuss how you both feel when you try your best.

   _____

   _____

   _____

Self-Control Home Page

Please hang this page on your refrigerator door and try using the skill of Self-Control in your home.

The Peacezone program is going great! We are now talking about the skill of **Self-Control.** We are learning how self-control can help us follow directions, stay safe, and control what we do and what we say. Your children are trying their best to help make our school safe and successful. Thanks for your support!

You can help your child learn about self-control by talking about how you and your child use the skill at home. Some parents have even found it helpful to use the word self-control *in a positive way with their children.*

Self-Control

▶ **Self-control is when I am in charge of what I do and what I say.**

▶ **I use my self-control to listen and follow directions.**

▶ **Using self-control helps me not do things that may be harmful to myself and others.**

▶ **Self-control helps me stay safe, be successful, and create peace.**

With your child, please answer the following questions. Have fun talking about self-control!

1. Read the description of self-control and discuss with your child how self-control can help both of you.

2. List how you and your child can use your self-control at home, at school, and in the community.

   _____   _____

   _____   _____

   _____   _____

3. List times you and your child did not use your self-control and discuss how you can learn from them.

   _____   _____

   _____   _____

   _____   _____

Thinking and Problem-Solving Home Page

Please hang this page on your refrigerator door and try using the skills of Thinking and Problem Solving in your home.

Students are learning to use the skill of **Thinking and Problem Solving** at home, at school, and in the community. When we have a problem to solve, instead of giving up, we need to keep thinking to find a solution. By thinking and problem solving, children are helping to create peace throughout our school.

Thinking and Problem Solving

► **Thinking is when I come up with as many ideas as I can.**

► **Problem solving is when I think in order to find the solution to a problem.**

► **I keep thinking until I solve the problem. I don't give up.**

► **Thinking and problem solving help me find ways to create peace.**

Imagine that you and your child are planning how to spend Saturday afternoon together; then answer the following questions.

1. Use your thinking and list all the different things you could do on Saturday afternoon.

_____   _____

_____   _____

_____   _____

_____   _____

2. Choose one activity you could do together and circle it.

3. Explain why you chose that activity.

_____

_____

_____

_____

Cooperation Home Page

Please hang this page on your refrigerator door and try using the skill of Cooperation in your home.

Your children are learning the skill of **Cooperation,** the final skill in the Peacezone program. To cooperate with others, children need to use the Pledge for Peace and all the Peacezone skills they have learned so far: Trying Your Best, Self-Control, and Thinking and Problem Solving. By cooperating to solve problems, children are helping to create peace at school, at home, and in the community.

Cooperation

▶ **Cooperation is when I work well with others.**

▶ **I cooperate to solve problems and resolve conflicts.**

▶ **Cooperation helps me create peace.**

With your child, think of one problem that you could cooperate on to solve. Some problems might involve household responsibilities, what to make for dinner, what movie to see, and so forth. Remember to practice using self-control to listen to each other, respect each other's ideas, give your opinion, and try your best to think of all the different ways you can solve the problem. Have fun cooperating!

1. Think of one problem that you could cooperate together to solve.

   _____

   _____

2. Cooperate to list all the different ways you could solve this problem.

   _____

   _____

   _____

3. Cooperate to solve the problem. What is the one solution to the problem that you both agree on?

   _____

   _____

Healing Skills: Activities and Resources

LeSette Wright

Teachers equip students with a variety of skills for life. Helping students to heal after loss, manage fear and anger, and resolve conflicts peacefully may reduce the prevalence of youth violence, delinquency, substance abuse, and related problems. Students who have been equipped with these skills show improved school attendance, greater academic success, and better overall functioning. Psychiatrists and psychologists use the Global Assessment of Functioning (GAF) Scale to measure overall psychological functioning (DSM-IV-TR; American Psychiatric Press, 2000). The GAF rates functioning on a scale from 0–100, with 100 being superior.

When our students learn the skills they need for life, they move toward a superior level of functioning. As you strive to help your students reach this goal, we recommend incorporating Peacezone healing skills with a GAF approach, interpreted in this context as grief and loss (G), anger (A), and fear management (F). The ability to manage grief, anger, and fear is a protective factor against negative outcomes and increases the likelihood that our students will move toward success.

Grief and Loss

Students experience loss in a variety of ways. Loss can result from the death or imprisonment of a loved one, divorce, addiction, relocation, or other factors. In 2001, homicide was the second leading cause of death for persons ages fifteen to thirty-four and the fourth leading cause of death for persons ages one to fourteen (Centers for Disease Control, 2003). According to the 2000 U.S. Census, 2.4 million grandparents were responsible for raising one or more of their grandchildren (U.S. Census Bureau, 2003). The U.S. Department of Justice (2000) reported that more than 721,000 parents to over a million children under the age of 18 were living behind bars. These statistics, and many more like them, provide a basis for estimating the numbers of children in our schools dealing with significant issues of grief and loss.

Children who are experiencing grief and loss can be overcome by feelings of fear and vulnerability. These feelings often influence their behavior throughout the day. Children express grief in a variety of ways, and sometimes they may appear to be unaffected by death or other losses. Very young children have difficulty understanding the permanency of death. Only after about age five do children experience grief in a form similar to that of adults.

Many situations and important events—such as holidays, the anniversary of a loved one's death, and September 11—may reawaken grief for students. Sometimes the pain of loss and trauma are triggered by small things, not recognized by others: the color of a person's shirt, a particular make of car, and certain sounds or smells, just to name a few. A kindergarten teacher tells the story of a student who would have tantrums while painting near the classroom window. She later learned that the student could see a red car from the window. The mother of this child had a batterer who drove a similar red car. Painting at the window in view of the red vehicle became a trigger for this child's classroom tantrums.

You can help your students during difficult times by making yourself available to talk and by using the opportunity to engage in a healing skills activity with your class. Grief varies from child to child, and it is important not to force communication but to listen and create a safe space. Helping children cope with loss enables them to heal and resume their lives more fully within their homes, schools, and communities. The Louis D. Brown story lays the foundation for healing within the curriculum. Please use the activities and resources described on the following pages for additional support.

Hands of Peace
Materials
Light purple construction paper; crayons, markers, pencils

Purpose
To develop healing skills in students while empowering them with a sense of help, hope, and healing in loss

Process

Have each student trace his or her hand on a piece of purple construction paper. Tell each student to write or indicate by drawing on the hand a way in which he or she could help a person who might be feeling the loss of someone that person loves.

After the students have finished, have them share what they wrote or drew on their hand outlines. You can then offer the students the option of giving their hand outlines to someone in their home, school, or community, or displaying them as an interconnected "peace ribbon" within your classroom or school.

Peace Café

Materials

Various, depending on the activities chosen

Purpose

To develop healing skills in students through creative expression

Process

Have students create a poem, song, dance, rap, painting, or dramatic presentation that promotes peace. Select a day and time when students can share their creative works with their classmates. Invite students to bring in snacks to share with the class.

This activity can be extended by inviting parents, administrators, and other students to view the presentations. You may also want to have your classroom present their works at a community center or facility for the elderly.

Anger Management

Anger is a normal human emotion that can range from mild irritation to intense rage. Like other emotions, anger causes changes in the body. You can tell when physical changes are occurring by observing a number of "red flags." Some of these red flags include clenched fists or teeth, rapid breathing or heart rate, yelling, extended silence, staring, and sweating. These physical changes are the body's way of telling us there is something wrong. Noting physical changes in yourself and your students will help you develop a classroom anger barometer (see the Peacemaking Barometer activity, which follows).

Anger usually results from loss, emotional pain, or fear. Loss of a loved one, having one's feelings hurt by teasing, or fear of failure in school are all common reasons for anger and acting-out behavior in students. Anger can be triggered by internal or external forces. A student could become angry at a classmate or at receiving a poor grade on a test, or the student's anger could be triggered by worrying about or memories of a traumatic event. Many of us are taught early in life that anger is bad and that people should not feel angry. Remind students that there is nothing wrong with feeling angry.

Peacemaking Barometer

Materials

Drawing paper, red and purple construction paper (or chalkboard and red and purple chalk)

Purpose

To help students understand and appreciate their ability to control their anger and be peacemakers

Process

Create two exclamation point–shaped barometers in your classroom on drawing paper or on a section of chalkboard. Put the words *unsafe* at the bottom and *safe* at the top. The purple peacemaking barometer will begin empty each day. The red anger barometer will begin full each day.

As students display peacemaking gestures, allow them to fill in a segment of the peacemaking barometer with the color purple. As students display angry gestures, allow them to remove a red segment of the anger barometer after they have used their self-control to calm down.

This activity will help students understand the significance of peacemaking, anger management, and self-control as daily responsibilities. It will also help them to visualize how their behavior affects the safety of their classroom.

Promoting Peace through Anger Release

Materials

Chalkboard; paper, markers, crayons

Purpose

To help students understand and appreciate positive expressions of anger and the usefulness of humor as an anger management tool

Process

Have students brainstorm ways that they can express their anger positively. Answers may include exercising, playing sports, singing, writing poetry, studying, helping someone in need, writing a letter, and so forth. Make a list of students' ideas on the chalkboard. After students have listed ten or more ideas, have them create a comic strip by making use of one of the brainstormed responses. Students may work in pairs or individually to create the comic strips.

When students have finished, have them share their comic strips with the class. Stress the importance of humor as an anger management tool. Remind students that taking situations or ourselves too seriously can lead to angry or violent outcomes.

As an extension of this activity, display the comic strips within the classroom, school, local library, or boys and girls club.

Fear Management

Like anger, fear is a normal emotion. The intensity of fear can range from mild apprehensiveness to extreme terror. Children express and respond to fear differently because the fear of objects and situations is often learned. Fear can be useful or harmful. A fear of being burned will keep a child from placing his hand in the fire, whereas a fear of failure may keep a child from trying her best.

Fear is the emotion that has been most studied. Scientists have learned that fear depends on very specific circuits, or pathways, in the brain. Studying the "fight or flight response" generated by fear, scientists have found that the brain processes information about threat and fear even when the person is not consciously aware of danger signals.

In *Maltreated Children: Experience, Brain Development and the Next Generation,* Dr. Bruce Perry (1996) discusses the impact of growing up in a persistently threatening environment on brain development in children. His research suggests that increased cell development in the brains of traumatized children may account for difficulties in learning, limited problem-solving abilities, and increased impulsive behaviors.

Most of these traumatized children fall on the higher end of intensity on the fear continuum. Understanding this continuum will help you to identify children who may require additional fear management strategies. Consulting the school counselor, school psychologist, or guidance department should be helpful in these situations.

Helping your students manage fear is important. The National Mental Health Association suggests the following ways to help children manage fear and violence: encourage children to talk, validate children's feelings, talk honestly about your own feelings, discuss safety procedures, create safety plans with your students, recognize behavior that may indicate a child is concerned about his or her safety, empower children, keep a dialogue going, and seek help when necessary. The Peacezone provides you with the framework to carry out these strategies. Please see the activities and resources described on the following pages for additional support.

Safety Shirts

Materials

Medium-sized T-shirt shapes cut from butcher paper or another type of heavy paper; crayons, markers, and pencils; safety pins or masking tape

Purpose

To empower students with a sense of security to help them manage their fears

Process

Have children brainstorm things that make them feel safe. Lead students in a discussion of why these items make them feel safe. After the discussion, pass out the precut "shirts" to your students. Have them draw or write on the shirts those things that make them feel safe. Laminate the shirts and keep them in a designated place within the classroom. Allow the students to wear their shirts when they need to by pinning or taping them to their clothes. (Keep in mind that students should not draw things on their shirts that would jeopardize the safety of others.)

Peaceful Words Story Ball

Materials

A ball

Purpose

To empower students to manage their fears by using peaceful words

Process

Have students sit in a circle on the floor. Remind them of the following part of the Pledge for Peace: "I will use peaceful words. Using words that are kind and friendly will help me create a peaceful home, school, and community." Explain that using peaceful words can help people when they are afraid.

Tell students that the class is going to create a story using peaceful words to help someone who is afraid. Show them the ball and tell them that it is a "peaceful words story ball." Explain that the story ball will help them create a story about overcoming fear with peaceful words.

Begin the story with a phrase such as "Once upon a time there was a little boy who was afraid to ride the school bus." Then roll the ball to a student, who will add to the story and roll the ball to the next student, who will add to the story, and so on.

After the story is finished, discuss how peaceful words in the story helped the boy deal with his fear. Ask the students if all the peaceful words came from others or if the boy told himself any peaceful words to help with his fear. Discuss how we can use peaceful self-talk to help us when we are afraid.

References and Resources

American Psychiatric Association. (2000). *Diagnostic and statistical manual of mental disorders* (4th ed., text rev.). Washington, DC: American Psychiatric Publishing.

Centers for Disease Control. (2003). *Web-based injury statistics query and reporting system* [Online]. National Center for Injury Prevention and Control, Centers for Disease Control and Prevention (producer). Retrieved from www.cdc.gov/ncipc/wisqars

Druck, K. (2003). *How to talk to your kids about school violence.* San Diego: The Jenna Druck Foundation.

Fried, S., & Fried, P. (1996). *Bullies and victims.* New York: M. Evans and Company.

Garbarino, J. (1995). *Raising children in a socially toxic environment.* San Francisco: Jossey-Bass.

Holmes, M., Mudlaff, S., & Pillo, C. (2000). *A terrible thing happened.* Washington, DC: Magination Press.

Oehlberg, B. (1996). *Making it better: Activities for children in a stressful world.* St. Paul: Redleaf Press.

Oliver, J., & Ryan, M. (2004). *Lesson One: The ABCs of life—The skills we all need but were never taught.* New York: Fireside Publishers.

Perry, B. D. (1996). *Maltreated children: Experience, brain development and the next generation.* New York: W.W. Norton.

Prothrow-Stith, D., & Spivak, H. (2004). *Murder is no accident: Understanding and preventing youth violence in America.* San Francisco: Jossey-Bass.

U.S. Census Bureau. (2003, October). *Grandparents living with grandchildren: 2000* [Online]. Retrieved from www.census.gov/prod/cen2000/doc/sf3.pdf, www.census.gov/population/www/socdemo/grandparents.html

U.S. Department of Justice, Bureau of Justice Statistics. (2000). *Special report: Incarcerated parents and their children* [Online]. Retrieved from www.ojp.usdoj.gov/bjs/pub/pdf/iptc.pdf

Books for Children of Incarcerated Parents

Butterworth, O. (1993). *A visit to the big house.* Boston: Houghton Mifflin.

I know how you feel because this happened to me. (n.d.). (Available from Center for Children with Incarcerated Parents, Pacific Oaks College and Children's Programs, 714 West California Blvd., Pasadena, CA 91105)

Just for you: Children with incarcerated parents. (n.d.). (Available from Center for Children with Incarcerated Parents, Pacific Oaks College and Children's Programs, 714 West California Blvd., Pasadena, CA 91105)

Two in every hundred: A special workbook for children with a parent in prison. (n.d.). (Available from Reconciliation, 702 51st Avenue North, Nashville, TN 37209)

Whitmore Hickman, M. (1984). *Last week my brother Anthony died.* Nashville: Abingdon Press.

Whitmore Hickman, M. (1990). *When Andy's father went to prison.* Niles, IL: Albert Whitman and Company.

Selected Web-Based Resources

School Safety and Violence Prevention Organizations

American Academy of Experts in Traumatic Stress:
www.schoolcrisisresponse.com

Centers for Disease Control and Prevention:
www.cdc.gov/ncipc/dvp/dvp.htm

Center for Effective Collaboration and Practice:
www.cecp.air.org

Center for the Prevention of School Violence:
www.ncsu.edu/cpsv

Center for Schools and Communities:
www.center-school.org

Center for the Study and Prevention of Violence:
www.colorado.edu/cspv

Communities against Violence Network:
www.askam.com/cavnet

Family Life Development Center:
www.child.cornell.edu

The Hamilton Fish Institute:
www.hamfish.org

Join Together:
www.jointogether.org

Keep Schools Safe:
www.keepschoolssafe.org

Keeping Schools and Communities Safe:
www.ed.gov/offices/oese/sdfs

National Alliance for Safe Schools:
www.safeschools.org

National Resource Center for Safe Schools:
www.safetyzone.org

National Mental Health Association:
www.nmha.org

Peacezone:
www.peacezone.org

General Child Development Organizations

American Academy of Pediatrics:
www.aap.org

American Association of School Administrators:
www.aasa.org

American Counseling Association:
www.counseling.org

American Federation of Teachers:
www.aft.org

American Psychiatric Association:
www.psych.org

American Psychological Association:
www.apa.org

American School Counselor Association:
www.schoolcounselor.org

Big Brothers Big Sisters:
www.bbbsa.org

Boy Scouts: www.boyscouts.org

Break the Cycle: www.break-the-cycle.org

Council of the Great City Schools:
www.cgcs.org

Council for Exceptional Children:
www.cec.sped.org

Dads and Daughters:
www.dadsanddaughters.org

Girl Scouts:
www.girlscouts.org

Kids-in-Mind—Movie Ratings That Really Work:
www.kidsinmind.com

The Media Project: www.themediaproject.com

National Association of Elementary School Principals: www.naesp.org

National Association of School Nurses: www.nasn.org

National Association of School Psychologists: www.nasponline.org/advocacy/youth violence

National Association of Secondary School Principals: www.nassp.org

National Education Association: www.nea.org

National Middle School Association: www.nmsa.org

National School Public Relations Association: www.nspra.org

School Social Work Association of America: www.sswaa.org

Southern Poverty Law Center: www.splcenter.org/news

Voices of Youth–UNICEF: www.unicef.org

Organizations Serving Victims and Survivors of Gun Trauma

Brady Campaign United with the Million Mom March: www.bradycampaign.org, www.millionmommarch.org

Brady Center to Prevent Gun Violence: www.bradycenter.org

Drive By Agony: www.drive-by-agony.org

Educational Fund to End Handgun Violence: www.gunfree.org

Gun Control Network: www.gun-control-network.org

Join Together (Gun Violence Project): www.jointogether.org/gv

Legal Community Against Violence: www.lcav.org

National Child Traumatic Stress Network: www.nctsnet.org

Peace Action Education Fund: www.webcom.com/peaceact

Physicians for Social Responsibility: www.psr.org

Violence Policy Center: www.vpc.org

Organizations Serving Victims and Survivors of Violence

American Association of Jewish Family Services:
www.ajfca.org

American Association of Suicidology:
www.suicidology.org

American Foundation for Suicide Prevention:
www.afsp.org

The Compassionate Friends, Inc.:
www.compassionatefriends.org

Mothers Against Violence in America:
www.mavia.org

Murder Victims' Families for Reconciliation:
www.mvfr.org/homepage.html

National Center for Victims of Crime:
www.ncvc.org

National Domestic Violence Hotline:
www.ndvh.org

National Organization of Victim Assistance:
www.try-nova.org

Neighbors Who Care:
www.neighborswhocare.org

Office for Victims of Crime:
www.ojp.usdoj.gov/ovc

Parents of Murdered Children, Inc.:
www.pomc.org

Tragedy Assistance Program for Survivors of Military Personnel:
www.taps.org

About the Authors

DEBORAH PROTHROW-STITH, M.D., is associate dean for faculty development and professor of public health practice at the Harvard School of Public Health. As a physician working in inner-city hospitals and neighborhood clinics, she recognized violence as a significant public health issue. In 1987, she established the first office of violence prevention in a state department of public health while serving as commissioner for the Department of Public Health for the Commonwealth of Massachusetts.

JOSEPH CHÉRY is co-founder of the Louis D. Brown Peace Institute, a center for peace education and survivors' outreach services. On December 20, 1993, Mr. Chery's fifteen-year-old son, Louis David Brown, was shot and killed while on his way to a Christmas party given by the group Teens Against Gang Violence. To honor their son's memory, Mr. Chéry and his wife, Clementina, founded the Louis D. Brown Peace Institute and developed the Louis D. Brown Peace Curriculum to teach the value of peace to elementary and high school students. The curriculum integrates reading, writing, classroom discussions, and community service to help students examine and understand the concepts of peacemaking and violence prevention.

JON OLIVER is a certified teacher who has spent thirty years developing Lesson One Company. He has frequently appeared in the national media and has made presentations at conferences and workshops around the country. His school reform efforts have earned him commendations from the White House. His book, *Lesson One: The ABCs of Life—The Skills We All Need but Were Never Taught,* has received endorsements from Bill Cosby, Marian Wright Edelman (president of the Children's Defense Fund), James Comer, M.D. (Yale University), and Alvin Poussaint, M.D. (Harvard University). He lives in Marblehead, Massachusetts.

CLEMENTINA CHÉRY is co-founder of the Louis D. Brown Peace Institute, a center for peace education and survivors' outreach services. The institute was founded in response to the random murder of her son, Louis D. Brown. Clementina Chéry is a founding member and past president of the National Coalition of Survivors for Violence Prevention. Mrs. Chéry is a full-time student at Springfield College, majoring in human services with a minor in criminal justice. She lives in Dorchester, Massachusetts.

Marci Feldman, MS.Ed., is a public health advisor with the National Center for Injury Prevention and Control at the U.S. Centers for Disease Control and Prevention. She is a certified school counselor, with several years' experience in that capacity in District of Columbia public schools. In addition to her school counseling experience, she has served as a crisis counselor, working with adults, families, and children.

Fern Shamis is assistant director of Lesson One Company and has been on the staff since 1986 as a teacher, curriculum developer, and administrator. She holds a master's degree in educational administration from Lesley University. Ms. Shamis has been responsible for overseeing all aspects of Lesson One Company's collaboration with the Peacezone project.